RISING CHINA
OPPORTUNITY OR STRATEGIC CHALLENGE

BASED ON PROCEEDINGS OF
NATIONAL SECURITY SEMINAR 2009
HELD AT USI, NEW DELHI
ON 25-26 NOV 2009

Established 1870

Published in association with
United Service Institution of India
New Delhi

Vij Books India Pvt Ltd
21 Ansari Road, Daryaganj, New Delhi

Published by

Vij Books India Pvt Ltd
(Publishers, Distributors & Importers)
4675-A, 21 Ansari Road
New Delhi - 110002
Phones: 91-11-43596460, 91-11- 65449971
Fax: 91-11-30126465
e-mail : vijbooks@rediffmail.com

ISBN: 978-93-80177-19-9

CONTENTS

S-54

RISING CHINA
OPPORTUNITY OR STRATEGIC
CHALLENGE

Edited By
Maj Gen P J S Sandhu (Retd)
Deputy Director and Editor, USI

PROCEEDINGS OF
National Security Seminar 2009

HELD AT
USI, NEW DELHI
ON
25-26 NOVEMBER 2009

Welcome Remarks

Lieutenant General PK Singh,
PVSM, AVSM (Retd), Director, USI of India

Air Commodore Jasjit Singh, distinguished panelists, excellencies, members of the United Service Institution of India (USI), members of the media, ladies and gentlemen. It is my privilege and honour to welcome you to this year's National Security Seminar on 'Rising China – An Opportunity or Strategic Challenge'.

Amongst the honoured guests, there are some who are here in USI for the first time. So, let me very briefly say something about the USI. It was founded in Simla in 1870. It is an autonomous and financially self supporting Institution with over 12,600 members. This Institution organised its first Lecture Seminar on 30th January 1871 – yes, 138 years ago! We discussed 'China' for the first time in 1889 and continue to do so even today. We at the USI have been looking at issues of interest to our members ever since we were founded.

China is a rising power. It has achieved tremendous progress in its economic development and has carved a place for itself as a leader in economic field. Based on China's economic success, the PLA has steadily promoted its modernisation programmes and this improved military capability is changing the military balance in the region. The increase in China's Comprehensive National Power (CNP) is evident, but what is not clear is – How China will use this growing power and influence in Asia and the World? Some of the questions that we thought needed answers were:-

(a) What are the goals of China's Security policies?

(b) How will China exercise its growing economic, political, military and soft power?

(c) Will China be a status quo power or a revisionist power?

(d) How can you build an enduring power equation in Asia?

Over the next two days, we will deliberate on these and many other issues. I would like to specially welcome the participants from China, the USA, Japan, South Korea, Philippines, Taiwan and of course India. I would also like to welcome the delegations from Okazaki Institute, Japan and the Cross Straits Prospect Foundation, Taiwan who are here to also participate in our bilateral dialogues. I must also extend a hearty welcome to the delegation from the Netherland's Advanced Defence Course led by Lieutenant General Diepenbrugge who have taken time off from their busy schedule to participate in this Seminar.

I am grateful to Air Commodore Jasjit Singh, AVSM, VrC, VM (Retd), Director Centre for Air Power Studies (CAPS) who has very graciously agreed to deliver the Keynote Address.

Air Commodore Jasjit Singh joined the Indian Air Force in 1954 as a fighter pilot and had a chequered career. He was awarded the Vir Chakra in 1971 Indo-Pak War. He was later the Director of Operations at the IAF Headquarters. He moved to Institute for Defence Studies and Analyses (IDSA), where he had an equally distinguished innings serving as its Director for 16 years. He was the Convenor of the Task Force to set up the National Security Council. He was awarded the Padma Bhushan by the President of India for outstanding service to the Nation in the field of defence and National security.

It is my privilege and honour to invite Air Commodore Jasjit Singh to now deliver the Keynote Address.

Keynote Address

Air Commodore Jasjit Singh, AVSM, VrC, VM (Retd)

Good morning ladies and gentlemen. I am indeed grateful to the Director, USI, Lieutenant General PK Singh for having asked me to share my views at such an important Seminar at USI. I must state this publicly that while I served with one think tank for pretty long time, in IDSA, and I started another think tank which has now completed 8 years, but my loyalties go to USI. I will give you a simple reason for this.

When we were Commissioned, we were simply made the members of USI. At that time a USI library catalogue was published and sent to us. I spent first five years of my Air Force service career at an airfield which is in the boon docks, in a place called Kalaikonda, where you could shoot panthers on the airfield but you could not find a book to read. Newspapers used to come a day late. So, the procedure at that time was that you could select two books from the catalogue and request USI to send them. You could keep them for one month. After you had finished reading, you posted them back at your cost to USI. I think some people may have forgotten to return books. Therefore, that process was stopped; which actually had been started by USI long time ago so that officers deployed in remote areas would have access to military related literature and everything that goes with it. When, I came to the Indian Air Force Headquarters for the first time in 1968, I could actively work with an outstanding human being, an outstanding officer and a long time Director of USI, Colonel Pyara Lal. So, to me it is homecoming; and as it happens at home, you can make many mistakes. If I do make any mistakes in this Keynote address, I hope you will understand that it is all because of my treating this more as an informal process.

I looked at the title, about the question, 'Rising China - an Opportunity or Strategic Challenge?'. One wishes that one could look at it from another angle also. If we change that word 'or' into 'and', it would read 'Opportunity and Strategic Challenge'. Then, I think we might be just a little closer to understanding what is going on, and what is going to happen in the future that would affect rest of the World, as also specifically India. India, because I tend to look at things from an Indian perspective. The choice whether this 'or' will change to 'and', actually depends on what time horizon you wish to look at. Are we looking at this year, next five years or the next twenty years or the next fifty years? Your answers may well be different. But you will still have one constant answer and that is, 'China is a rising power'. I also don't believe that China's rise to power is going to be disrupted in any way. There is a lot of wishful thinking, somewhere in the West mostly, that something in China will implode because it has now additional internal problems. I heard much more of this in early 1990's, when actually China was nervous. Why I say this is because in my previous incarnation I used to go to China with strong contacts with think tanks in China - between IDSA, and Chinese Strategic Institute for Research (CSIR), and National Defence University (NDU).

When the Soviet Union collapsed and the American pressures built up all round, I think there was an uncertainty, amounting to almost essential vulnerability in the Chinese mind to say that the next turn for destabilisation of a country from outside sources, led by the USA, would be that of China. Therefore, at that time they welcomed much closer relationship with India. Although, chronologically it starts with Prime Minister Rajiv Gandhi's visit in 1988, but by 1987 in fact, the Chinese literature was starting to talk about: Indian Armed Forces are highly professional – there is lot to learn from them. That is before the Tiananmen square incident. After 1989, that added to their uncertainties creating a sense of weakness and vulnerability.

As time went by and once we got rapid access to Soviet military design base, one major item for which they had no answer upto that time was: How to modernise the Chinese military? Because everything was based on the original Soviet designs, there was no way they could do it, except through reverse engineering – but they just could not do it. And Soviets were not willing to help them. In late 1980's, as the Gorbachev's policies got going, they said that they were improving relations with China, and also helping in upgrading the industries. It was asked of the Soviets, *'Are you going to upgrade their Defence industry?'* The answer used to be a categorical - 'No'. We don't want to create a threat for ourselves for the future.

Now, right or wrong, this perception had to be put aside because with the collapse of the Soviet Union came a tremendous amount of economic crisis. That allowed what was to follow. Here comes the first difference of approach and method. India simply ignored that strategic opportunity, inspite of a much closer relationship with the Soviet Union in those days, when 80 per cent of our weapons were ex-Soviet design base. Not one Soviet technologist, engineer, designer was brought into India. However, this issue of the 5th generation fighter aircraft design jointly is a much later happening and I don't know the future of that.

Coming back to the theme of this Seminar, I want to say first what I should be saying at the end. Let me begin by answering the question, 'Rising China, is it an opportunity or a strategic challenge?' The answer will depend mainly on how China conducts itself in the future, Chinese perceptions of what is happening in the world and their world view. Some of it, we do have an understanding, and that could change as time goes by. Lot of people will talk about this as a Middle Kingdom syndrome. Perhaps, a little bit of that will influence, a little bit of Sun Tzu will influence and a little bit of something else will also influence. However, having been to China for 13 years regularly, twice or thrice a year, and the Chinese coming here to IDSA; I at least got the impression that the Chinese, like us, have an old civilization. So many things are deeply rooted in that civilization, like ours. But in other terms, what they do generally, will not be too far away from the basic civilizational values that they have, regardless of the political system in many other cases.

So, in this context, what is the landscape? First, there is a global power shift going on from the West to the East. It is only a *'return'* of power to the East. It is not something new that is happening except that those who do not read history may not know it. What does that history tell us? Today serious literature, and I think all the data tells us that, global power shift from the West to the East is taking place essentially because of the rise of China and India. If you take a more detailed look, then you say, yes, China is well ahead of India in that process. In fact, not that far ahead, compared to what I am going to say in terms of historical experience.

At the beginning of the 18th Century, just two countries manufactured approximately 60 per cent of the world's manufacturing output. These two countries also contained 62 per cent of the World's total income or GDP, as you today calculate. Which were these two countries? Number one was China which accounted for 33 per cent, second was India at 24 per cent.

Then, 'industrialisation' in the West, the 'Industrial Revolution' which actually started in England and then spread to Europe and North America, became the cause of many things – not only India becoming a colony, and China being badgered and humiliated, as the Chinese say, by these powers, where even a small power like Belgium had a huge empire in Africa. All that came out of the Industrial Revolution. In that process, the older method of economic productivity was destroyed. India and China, both, were de-industrialised. I wish I could show you my favourite graph, where both just keep coming down roughly parallel to each other, till by 1950, India was exporting just 0.6 per cent of the global manufacturing output. It has now moved upto close to 2 per cent. The Chinese had come down to 2.1 per cent and moved upto 6 per cent of the global output. Now, the two graphs are again rising. Inevitably, some other countries' graphs are coming down. So, if we look into the future, this is inevitable and this is not just the National Informatics Centre (NIC) report. This is something that you could look into upto 20 years ago. This is the reality, from that point of time. If that is so, then one conclusion is that Indians need not bother too much about China, or not lose sleep over it. I do not lose sleep that China is ahead of us. It was always ahead of us in some areas, like manufacturing etc. In terms of income and economic capability, it is ahead of us today – it will remain ahead of us. It is not the end of everything when you consider a nation, a power and international relationships.

The second is, 'What sort of international system are we seeing that is evolving or is there?' We learnt a lot. We were told that the world was bi-polar during or when the Cold War was on. I could never understand that fully. Thirty eight countries on one side and thirteen countries on the other side, and 148 outside it, do not make the World bi-polar. India and China remained outside it, inspite of the early years of the Soviet-China military alliance. By the late 1950's, it was very clear that they were no longer working together. In fact, all declassified documents tell us that the leadership was privately almost abusive to each other. Whatever the World was, we want to know what the World is today, and which way it is going in this landscape? Where does China fit in and how will China deal with that international system? One view is that the World is becoming multi-polar. There are countries who want the world to become multi-polar. The leading countries that are seeking multi-polarity are China, Russia, France and some of the others. Many Indians talk about multi-polarity because we don't like the word uni polar. Bi-polar is finished, I am not too sure whether multi-polarity is the right term. What then is the right term that we would like to see in the future?

I think the reality today is still that the world is poly centric. A large number of centres of power, some bigger some smaller, but in a globalised world what you see is strictly speaking a poly centric world. But the difference is that when China talks about multi-polarity, what comes out of many writings and statements is in fact that multi-polarity at the global level will be based on uni-polar Asia, with China at the head. Because from that perspective only it can match up to the United States which still runs, not a uni-polar World, but a uni-polar system of the Euro-Atlantic countries. You have here, not very complex but essentially two clear set of countries, not blocs – because they have an intense economic, social and other connections with each other. So, you are not going to see the return of a Cold War, certainly not the type that existed before. But you see here a different type of an international model that will emerge. What emerges, will depend on 'major powers' who will have that influence and the 'thinkers' who will think about this in a greater or lesser degree.

China's belief at the moment is that the US policies are trying to contain it. The US believes that China is a future problem area, not a threat; yet, with whom they must cooperate. I believe that China is trying to undermine the US power so that its own rise in international system is facilitated. In that undermining of the United States, it gets very uncomfortable and wants to do lots of things with those countries with whom the US seeks better relationship. I will give you two examples a little later.

What is happening specifically to China itself, is important. We all tend to look at this economic growth and infrastructure and such things that go on. I wonder that how much of that infra structure that one saw, stands today. There was a time when I took 2½ hrs drive to reach from Beijing to the Great Wall. Just seven years later, it took me just 45 minutes to get to the same place, because of the type of infrastructure that is coming up now. Perfectly good buildings on the Main Street of Beijing were pulled down and re-built so that now they look completely modern. Not just in Beijing but also in the outlying cities. That is yet to percolate down into the rural areas. I am not talking about the political system. I will leave that out for the time being because that itself has strong impact on many things.

But it did 'acquire', as it started to modernise particularly. It 'acquired' the East Coast. The area to the east of the Great Wall started to become prosperous and affluent in the beginning. And in the process, with their traditional ability, China started to invest a lot more into the 'periphery' at that time which is still within the Chinese territorial boundary i.e. Tibet and Xingjian. They thought that they had actually now assimilated and controlled the old periphery, which now became part of the new core, and therefore they stepped out ahead of that. Ahead of that, at different times, then is Central Asia. While Obama said Af-Pak, I would say, for China it is Pak-Af. Pakistan from the very beginning, from 1950's in fact, has been a strong one. The reasons were very clear. We in India tend to believe that the Chinese are doing this to raise a counter to India, perhaps they may have had some such thought about containment of India, and therefore Pakistan is a part of that. I don't think that is really true. I am not saying that it is not part of the process. But I think that is not the major reason as to why China started to support Pakistan, to the extent of giving nuclear weapons, nuclear material and missiles – eighty per cent of weapons of Pakistan military are of Chinese origin. The Chinese weapons are now high technology, so Pakistan now also gets high technology weapons. The reason is to give Pakistan a degree of autonomy from the US influence. Therefore, when the influence is increased, the Chinese just step back a little, and wait it out. You know very well that the US history runs on a four year cycle. With every change of the President, you will have things changing and you get new opportunities. Pakistan in the last 50 years has been the 'Frontline' state three times. The other three times, it has been under 'severe sanctions'. So that is the fluctuating type of relationship that the United States has with others.

The Chinese maintain a steady constant relationship at a little odd level, but substantive. If you ask the Pakistanis, they will tell you that China is an all weather friend. And, they have been so. Although, China when it agreed in 1965 to provide weapons, after asking a question to say, 'Are you serious about fighting?' When they were told yes, they said alright, in that case we will help. But when Ayub Khan flew down on a secret mission on 19th September, during the 1965 war to Beijing, with a request that China should step up its pressure on India and the border, the Chinese actually told them that at the highest level that 'you must keep fighting'. And, if you are losing on the plains, go back into the hills. Their own model of Mao's people's war is what was advocated. Of course, one view is that Sandhurst qualified Field Marshal had not particularly liked the idea of going back to the hills and fighting a guerilla warfare for an endless period of time, because there was nothing internal, really speaking in this case. But that is what it is.

The US relationships, the US policies, therefore, have a major bearing on how China's rise is going to be. Is it likely to be an opportunity or a challenge? It does not mean that countries like India should not have a closer relationship with the US. But to be conscious of the fact, that as long as we understand that the Chinese 'grand strategy' is focused on the United States as a point of reference. Therefore, the US policies and its relationship with other countries, which could add to that power or subtract from that power, that becomes then the rational method of the Chinese looking at the World, and also their own rise.

The periphery as I mentioned has been shifting further and further. So, if the periphery includes our neighbourhood like Bangladesh, Myanmar – Pakistan of course is a de-facto ally, that periphery has now gone much further. This is an old dream of the Chinese, which goes back to perhaps the earlier part of the 20th Century definitely. But certainly, after PRC came into being to be the leader of the World, if possible; if that was not possible, to be the leader, at that time in 1950's of the Afro Asian world. That is where India was the competitor. In fact China could not rise upto it, and that upset Mao Tse Tung extremely. From that perspective, therefore, he developed a slight amount of personal dislike for the Indian Prime Minister who had charisma and everything else. Mao could not understand why Nehru got so much attention, despite his many achievements. Not only in

Afro Asian thing, but also in the Non Aligned movement, they could not find a foothold. In 1991, in our discussion, I told the State Secretary of China, "Since you pursue an independent policy, why don't you sit in the Non-Aligned movement?" He said, "we are thinking of joining as an observer." So we have a choice on siding on a specific issue rather than anything else. In last two decades we have seen what was periphery – incorporated fully into China, or it was believed that it was fully incorporated and assimilated, i.e. Tibet and Xingjian. Events of the last year, and this year indicate that it is not so. While it remains within the boundaries of China's territories, this is a problem that is going to take a long time to solve. This is likely to be one of the fault lines between China and India.

The Chinese look at it only from their perspective. Indians, by and large also tend to look at it from other side's perspective, a little more than our own side of the perspective. But, when you get these out of the way and see what the reality is, at least my view is, and I have talked to my Chinese friends again and again over the last 18 years: 'Kindly create conditions that these 1,80,000 (Tibetan) refugees can go back, at least those who want to go back. They are the people who belong to Tibet. Many of them want to go back. There was an agreement between India and China in 1954, that culture etc would be promoted, not changed. Whereas these refugees, who are virtually in their second generation, could be a potential flash point in future, which the Government of India may not be able to control. It may not even know when it starts. I think, we need to think over this very carefully because, I certainly did not expect that there would be disturbances in Tibet, of the type as we saw last year. We find that even in Xingjian, the call came from Turkey that legal rights must be maintained. Why? Going back to the ancient Turkey linkages – not Islamic linkages incidentally. Islamic linkage in Xingjian is actually from Pakistan, which the Chinese have opposed and stopped. The only time that they got a little annoyed with Pakistan was on that issue.

There is one other point I want to say about the word 'strategic challenge' before I get to the end of it. This is a term that I used the day I became

Director, IDSA, it happened to be a day, when the Press was present and I did say, "China is India's long term strategic challenge". And 22 years later, I am willing to repeat that. China is India's strategic challenge. Unfortunately, the press next morning said, "The new Director IDSA says, China is a new threat." I find a great difference between a 'challenge' and a 'threat'. I had a Senior Colonel of the PLA in a conference in 1999 in Sweden, holding forth to say that India says that, *"China is a threat, they are lying"* and all such things. That officer was full of *'josh'*. So, finally I had to tell him with the Swedish Prime Minister sitting in the Chair, *"I don't think, we think that you are a threat. You are not a threat because we will make sure that, unlike 1962, you don't become a threat. Well, all that we have to do is to defend ourselves."* Please understand that China is not a threat; China is a potential challenge.

Now that China's military is growing in a massive way, people are forgetting that once you have this immense infusion of high technology into a system, how far the Chinese military system will be able to absorb that technology and use it is still a question mark. I will put another 5 to 10 years. But in terms of systems, there is no dearth of it. Whichever ones or sources you look today, this is so. 96 per cent of their weapons, including nuclear weapons and missiles, have no relevance for a country which is far away. People talk about power projection. That power projection is still being limited to the sea, to a certain distance, where in any case they claim many islands. It's not so much power projection but a change in doctrine and changing strategy, in line with their expectations from the new military technologies. For example, China's White Paper of 19 December 2004, categorically says very officially and clearly, that we are planning to fight a local border war, which is very logical and that we are going to win that local border war with command of the 'sea' and command of the 'air' and the use of the *'strategic forces'*. The army will be reduced and streamlined basically for defence. The term, 'command of the air', was last used in 1923. Even the United States does not use that sort of language today. This is the official Chinese White Paper on Defence, we are not talking of scholar's point of view or interpretations. I don't even have to interpret this. 'Command of the Sea' again is something that people like Mahan and people like Gorshkov had talked of. No modern countries are talking of this. This is one Country which is talking of this. This is the way we are going to keep limited the local border war, but on the ground; in the air we will go on the offensive and defensive. How many countries will be able to withstand this type of military pressure. No country can stand the type of military pressure that the United States is capable of exercising. Let us leave the United States out. But, China certainly runs at 'Number two' power in the World, economically and otherwise and now as a military power. In Asia, it is the biggest military, biggest military spender, and now has the most recent technology into it. To give a very simple example. India one day, in about 10-12 years from today, will have 210 Sukhoi 30's, China today has 400, will go on to have 450 in the next two years. So, that is the kind of scale that we are talking about. We have the first Airborne Early Warning System (AWAC), the Israelis delivered to us a few months ago – they have five of them already in use, and one of them has already been transferred to Pakistan. One could go on but I do not want to talk about their military capability. They are very clear on this issue. There used to be some confusion amongst the scholars earlier because when the original form of modernisation was written, the military modernisation appeared at 'Number Four'. This was interpreted wrongly in my view, and I kept arguing at that time that this is not the 'sequence'. These are just four items. You cannot modernise a military unless you have a strong enough economy. Military systems do not come free anymore, even by the superpower. Therefore, everything else is linked in a more continuous manner.

As far as new things are concerned, they have already improved; but their nuclear arsenal has not changed basically in the last 30 years. What has changed is the ability to create and shoot down Satellites in the air. It will have vast impact on the nature of future war, which is tending to shift more and more reliance on 'Space'. Only three countries like the USA, Russia and China, which have an anti Satellite capability, demonstrate it.

They have also gone into what Blue Ribbons Commissioner of the US had actually suggested to the American President way back in 1988, that with the accuracies that we are getting on our ballistic missiles, we should be able to start thinking of using the ballistic missiles with conventional warheads. Not much attention was paid to this Commission by the United States. It was strange, because normally Blue Ribbon Commissions have to be implemented, but the Chinese have learnt their lesson. About a thousand of such missiles are deployed on to Taiwan. The impact of the conventional missiles is actually much more psychological and political, than mere kinetic. Although with higher accuracy, you can target a very specific area. About 15000 missiles have been fired in wars since 1943 and everytime they were used, there was enormous impact on the political psychological side and also on the military side. We talk a great deal about 1991 Gulf War. The United States and its allies flew about 1,17,000 combat sorties during that War. 16 per cent of those sorties were aimed at finding and hitting the *'scuds'*. The largest quantum of air effort was spent in that war was on *'scuds'*. Iraq fired 87 of them with questionable results. They knocked off many fixed launching sites. They did not get a single mobile launcher – not even one. 16 per cent of 1,17,000 combat sorties is a fair amount of effort with the highest capable aircraft that they had.

So the signals are very clear. The neighbours better look out, think what you want to do about it. Therefore, there comes a question. In the last few years, one finds the Chinese statements and Chinese actions to be a lot more assertive than what they were earlier. How do I see it? That's roughly my ending point. Because, the first half of 1990's, they were very nervous. But now they are clearly very assertive towards India. Let's just talk of China-India. At that time, they went into two agreements – 1993 and 1996. They are not denying them, but they are not moving for any action on those. What was agreed upon between China and India was that we would try and solve the border issues but meanwhile lets demarcate the Line of Actual Control (LAC). Now from 1993, it is 2009 – there is very little movement. We can't demarcate the LAC because the Chinese are not very keen on it. You are not going to get a solution on the boundary and the territorial question any time soon.

I have two propositions here. First is the question, which I keep asking, 'Why can't we demarcate the Line of Actual Control?' It is difficult on the Himalayas, but certainly not if we try. A wonderful answer was given for the first time by a very senior person in the Government in Beijing. I had pressed him for the answer, saying that people ask me this question as Director, IDSA. Why don't you get on with this? Are we not moving sufficiently or are the Chinese not serious about it? His answer to me was, *"Mr Singh, it's going to take a long time."* I asked, if he would like to share the reason with me? *He said, "Yes. The trouble in your Country is that your Government keeps changing too fast."* I said, certainly it changes every 5 years by and large. But are you waiting for a Government that will last 20 years before you actually demarcate the LAC. You knew this, even when you signed the Agreement. You signed the Agreement because at that time you wanted to appear friendly with India and, therefore, India meant much at that time. We were under sanctions from the United States, so we looked like an obvious 'Number two' to the leader. India is 'Number three' country in the World today. And in next 20 years, the Russian and European population is going to go down completely, the Japanese is going down rapidly, the Chinese will go down a little bit but they have a large population, like us. India is still increasing its population although not at the same rate at what we were earlier. That makes it a problem. All I would say is that, I see no evidence, and experts are sitting here from both sides from China and India, I don't see any incentive for China to settle the boundary question, nor any incentive to demarcate the LAC. If I read my history right, the Sino-Soviet-Russian border problems have existed for 170 odd years. This is a problem that is only 60 years old. So, let us wait for 100 years. We are both old civilizations, we can manage. The more we talk about solving the border dispute, we are actually giving a leverage to Beijing to make some little effort to raise the level a little bit. We never heard Tawang being part of the problem in the last 45 or 50 years. Where did it come from? If they wanted

Tawang in 1962, they could have stopped just at Tawang, rather than carrying onto Mc Mahon Line, while criticising Mc Mahon Line.

Under these conditions, the second problem is that I have been trying to re-look at the 1962 War. Three or four books have been published by the Chinese on the War. I hope somebody can help us in understanding what is written there. Unfortunately, and I hope I am wrong, that this recent assertiveness ties up chronologically at least with a fact that India-US relations have come much closer. In fact, you can go back to 2003, and then 2005. After which, raising strategic partnership, actually there has been additional pressures from the Chinese side. Part of that rise in pressure has been because this is the period when India-US relations have actually improved. There are also pressures on India and many other countries because the US influence and control in Pakistan is increasing. Pakistan is in a state of instability. So, while the US is there for a variety of reasons, which would serve the interest of everybody, especially if the nuclear weapons can be kept under control by somebody –Pakistan Army, we hope!!

So here is a stable rising India; and a declining economy, a declining society in Pakistan next door – both close to the United States from a totally different perspective. In both cases, China sees a problem and therefore, needs to do something. Therefore, options for India, under these circumstances are fairly clear. There is a word that I feel has been grossly understood – 'Non Alignment'. But that is a word that explains what the best option for India ought to be; the United States on one side and China on the other side. Because 'Non Alignment' is different from 'Non Aligned Movement'. My understanding of history is that this term was accepted by the Indian political leadership, at least for the Congress, not the Muslim League, in 1938. It is not the product of the Cold War. That again doesn't mean neutrality either. We can say, strategic autonomy. We can use any other word you like. But India is also placed in a unique position to be able to deal with China's rise, not in opposition to it, but in working with it. So there is an area where we can have sufficient cooperation. *While we address our own specific challenge, which is Comprehensive National Development which no elected government can ignore.* Under the circumstances, therefore, China's rise is to be welcomed and strategic challenge has to be understood. I think we are capable of doing that.

To encapsulate that into just two words, 'India should seek to have a policy of cooperation with China, which is in force; but at the same time, cooperate but 'insure'? How does that 'insurance' come in? You have a credible deterrent available. So, you have 'insurance' partly for that purpose. The infra structure being improved in the Himalayas, the Chinese are complaining about it. They expect that while they are building these beautiful railway lines all the way, and they plan to build more railway lines, that we are not watching and what are the implications of those things? Our aim should be; Number one, to avoid any potential conflict or clashes with China, not by 'giving in' anything, but to maintain the 'status quo' on the frontiers. For which the answer lies in the demarcation of LAC. You can even forget about it for a long time. We have the Chief of the General Staff, PLA saying in 1998, *"This is going to take a long time."* That's that. So why do we need to go on and on. I think we should stop even this bilateral dialogue on the borders. Because if it is non productive, then minor concessions given here and there will not improve things. That will make things worse in the long term.

China is a marvelous country, wonderful people, I have lots and lots of friends there but governments don't run on simple personal friendships. They work on National interest. Our National interest and values are different. That doesn't mean that we would be in conflict. What we need is that we need to understand this much more. I certainly take great pleasure in China's rise because its visible and I have seen it happening from end 1989, till the last time I went there in 2002. It is great for a developing country that only 20 years earlier, before they started modernisation, they were in the middle of the cultural revolution and what it caused. At the same time, China must recognise that there are other civilizations too.

Now on the lighter side, I would like to end by saying one more thing. In early 1970's there was a book, which I picked up because its title caught my eye: '*India, China and the Ruins of Washington*'. The thesis propounded in the book is: Because the US had just opened upto China at that time in 1971-72, this scholar was trying to caution the Americans to say, '*Hold on. Open a book of History of China at the halfway point and you will get to the Third Century BC. Open a book on Indian history, you will certainly come up to Third or Fourth Century AD. If you open a book on the US history, you may be lucky if you can open it at the Civil War.*'

Thank you everybody.

PARTICIPANTS

Lieutenant General PK Singh, PVSM, AVSM (Retd) was commissioned into 2 Field Regiment (SP) Artillery on 16 December 1967. He retired as General Officer Commanding-in-Chief South Western Command on 31 August 2008. He participated in 1971 Indo-Pak War and was the Deputy Director General MI (Foreign Division) during Operation Vijay. He assumed charge as the Director of the United Service Institution of India, New Delhi on 1 January 2009.

Air Commodore Jasjit Singh, AVSM,VrC,VM (Retd) joined the Indian Air Force in 1954 and retired in 1988. He served as the Director of Operations of the Indian Air Force, before being deputed to the Institute for Defence Studies and Analyses, New Delhi, where he was Director from 1987 to 2001. Founder Director of the Centre for Strategic and International Studies, he currently heads Centre for Air Power Studies, New Delhi.

Shri MK Rasgotra, IFS (Retd) was a Member of the Punjab Education Service till September 1949, when he entered Indian Foreign Service. His tenure as Foreign Secretary from 1982 to 1985 was marked by a renewal of Indo-American relations, sustained negotiations with Pakistan and a tentative opening to China. He was member of the UN Disarmament Advisory Board from 1983-1990. In recognition of his long service to the Nation, he was honoured with Padma Bhushan in 2002.

Lieutenant General VR Raghavan,PVSM,UYSM,AVSM (Retd) had a distinguished career in the Indian Army and retired as Director General of Military Operations. His combat experience included operations in wars with Pakistan and China, and in counter-insurgency campaigns. He joined the Delhi Policy Group as the founding Director. Presently, he is President, Centre for Security Analyses and has been appointed Adviser of the newly constituted International Commission on Nuclear Non-Proliferation and Disarmament.

Professor Zhang Guihong is the Executive Director of the Centre for South Asian Studies and the Centre for UN Studies at the Institute of International Studies of Fudan University. He is a Council member of China's Association of South Asian Studies, China-India Friendship Association, United Nations Association of China and Vice President of Association of Asian Scholars in China. His major areas of research are Sino-US-Indian relations, International Organisations and Asia-Pacific security.

Professor   Srikant Kondapalli, JNU is an Associate Professor in Chinese Studies at Jawaharlal Nehru University. He is also an Honorary Fellow at Institute of Chinese Studies, Delhi and Research Associate at the Centre for Chinese Studies, University of Stellenbosch, South Africa. He served at Institute for Defence Studies and Analyses, New Delhi for 12 years. He learnt Chinese language at Beijing language and Culture University and was a post-Doctoral Visiting Fellow at People's University, Beijing from 1996-98. He was also a Visiting Professor at National Chergchi University, Taipei in 2004 and a Visiting Fellow at China Contemporary International Relations, Beijing in May 2007.

Lieutenant General (Army) Masahiro Kunimi (Retd) is the Special Adviser Ocean Policy Research Foundation in Tokyo, Japan. He was the First Director General of Cabinet Satellite Intelligence Centre, Cabinet Office from April 2001 to March 2005. He served as the First Director General of Defence Intelligence Headquarters, Ministry of Defence from January 1997 to December 1999.

Vice Admiral KK Nayyar, PVSM,AVSM (Retd) is a former Vice Chief of the Indian Navy. He commanded both the Western and Eastern Fleets of the Indian Navy. He also served as Flag Officer Commander-in-Chief, Southern Naval Command. Post retirement he has been closely associated with a number of think tanks dealing with international security issues. He is the Founder President of National Maritime Foundation and the Forum for Strategic and Security Studies, New Delhi. Currently, he is a Member of the National Security Advisory Board.

Shri Mohan Guruswamy has wide ranging professional experience of 30 years. It includes teaching at the John F Kennedy, School of Government, Harvard University, Northeastern University Business School, Boston and the Administrative Staff College of India, Hyderabad. He was Adviser to the Finance Minister, Government of India (1998-99) holding the rank of Secretary on economic and financial issues. Presently, he is the Chairman of Centre for Policy Alternatives, New Delhi, an independent think tank focussed on policy analysis.

Ms Bethany Danyluk is an Associate at Booz Allen Hamilton, a USA based strategy and consulting firm. She is a member of the International Institute for Strategic Studies and Women in International Security. She serves as a Managing Director of Finance for Young Professionals in Foreign Policy .

Professor Aileen Baviera is currently Professor of Asian Studies at the Asian Centre, University of Philippines. She was the Dean of the Asian Centre (September 2003-October 2009) and Head of the Centre for International Relations and Strategic Studies of the Philippine Foreign Institute (1993-1998) and Executive Director of Philippines-China Development Resource Centre (1998-91). She lectures regularly at the Foreign Service Institute and the National Defence College, Philippines.

Shri Jayadeva Ranade (Retd) is a former Additional Secretary, Cabinet Secretariat, Government of India. He is a seasoned China analyst with over 25 years experience in the field. His foreign assignments have included Beijing and Hong Kong. His last foreign posting, prior to retirement in late 2008, was as a Minister in the Indian Embassy in Washington. He is presently a Distinguished Fellow with the Centre for Air Power Studies.

Rear Admiral KR Menon (Retd) was a submarine specialist in the Indian Navy. He retired in 1994 as the Assistant Chief of the Naval Staff (Operations). He has participated in military CBM talks with neighbouring countries and was in the first military delegation to Pakistan. He was also a Member of the Arun Singh Committee to restructure the National Defence set up in India and a Member of National Defence University Committee. He is currently the Chairman of the Task Force on Net Assessment and Simulation in the National Security Council.

Professor Han Hua is an Associated Professor and Director at the Centre for Arms Control and Disarmament at the School of International Studies at Peking University, China. She is an expert on International Arms Control and Disarmament Politics, Foreign Policies in South Asian Countries and US Politics and Foreign Policy in Asia Pacific region.

Professor Michael Pillsbury was educated at Standard University and Columbia University. He studied bureaucratic politics with Roger Hilsman, President Kennedy's Intelligence Director at the State Department. During the Reagan administration he was the Assistant Under Secretary of Defence for Policy Planning and responsible for implementation of the programme of covert aid known as the Reagan Doctrine. In 1975-76, his proposal at the RAND Corporation, that the USA should establish intelligence and military ties with China was publicly commended by Ronald Reagan, Henry Kissinger and James Schlesinger. Later, that became the US policy during the Carter and Reagan administrations.

Mr Yung Sheng Chao holds a bachelors degree from Fu Hsing Kang College and Masters in Oral communication from Kansas University and CSIS,USA. His dissertations include International Security and Military Strategy, 2003; Peaceful-Rise Strategy in China, 2004;The Reliance and Balance of the USA, China and Taiwan, 2005; and The Assessment of

Military Strategy between Taiwan and China, 2006. He has participated in numerous seminars and conferences on National Security and Military Strategy of the USA and China.

Lieutenant General (Air Force) Takayoshi Ogawa (Retd) was commissioned in the Japan Air Self Defence Force (JASDF) in March 1973. He specialised as an Air Weapons Controller. He is a graduate of the US Air Command and Staff College, Maxwell AFB and the National Institute for Defence Studies, Japan Defence Agency. He obtained Masters degree in National Strategy and Security Studies from the US National War College. He retired from JASDF in December 2007 as Commander, Air Development and Test Command. Presently, he is General Adviser with the Electronics Products and System and Group, Mitsubishi Electric Company.

Colonel (now Brigadier) Subodh Kumar was commissioned into Army Air Defence in June 1982. He is a graduate of Defence Services Staff College, Wellington and Higher Defence Management Course, College of Defence Management, Secunderabad. He commanded 142 Air Defence Regiment (SP). He was Senior Research Fellow at USI of India and carried out research on issues related to militarisation of the outer Space. Presently, he is Commander 786 (I) AD Brigade.

Shri K Raghunath, IFS (Retd) joined the Indian Foreign Service in 1962. After having held many diplomatic and other important assignments during his long and distinguished career, he became India's Foreign Secretary in 1997, and later was India's Ambassador to Russia in 2001. Prior to becoming the Foreign Secretary, he was Secretary (East) from 1995-1997, in the Ministry of External Affairs, in which capacity he was handling West Asia and dealing with Israel directly.

Vice Admiral Hideaki Kaneda (Retd) is a Director for the Okazaki Institute and a Trustee of Research Institute of Peace and Security. He was a Senior Fellow of Asia Centre and JF Kennedy School of Government of the Harvard, and a Guest Professor of Faculty of Policy Management of

Keio University. He served in the Japan Marine Self Defence Force from 1968 to 1999.

Professor Jaeho Hwang received his PhD in International Relations from the London School of Economics. He is a Research Fellow at the Centre for Security and Strategy within the Korean Institute for Defence Analyses. He is now a Visiting Research Fellow at Yonei University and Kyungnam University, and was earlier a Visiting Research Fellow at University of Leeds, China Foreign Affairs and University of Melbourne.

Professor Sujit Dutta holds the Mahatma Gandhi Chair at the Nelson Mandela Centre for Peace and Conflict Resolution, Jamia Millia University, Delhi. Till May 2009, he was Senior Fellow and Head of the East Asian Studies at the Institute for Defence Studies and Analyses (IDSA), New Delhi. He has been a member of the India-China Eminent Persons Group (2001-2005) and the National Security Council Task Force on China (2006-07). He was a Senior Fellow at the United States Institute of Peace, Washington DC (1997-98).

Shri Shiv Shankar menon, IFS (Retd) started his career with Indian Foreign Service in 1972. He has served with distinction in every portfolio held by him at the Ministry of External Affairs and in the Indian embassies in Beijing , Vienna and Tokyo. Later, he was an Adviser to the Atomic Energy Commission. He has been Indian Ambassador to China and Israel and High Commissioner to Sri Lanka. He is a former Foreign Secretary of India. Currently he is the National Security Adviser.

RISE OF CHINA

FIRST SESSION

Chairman	Shri MK Rasgotra, IFS (Retd)
First Paper	Lieutenant General V R Raghavan, PVSM,UYSM,AVSM (Retd)
Second Paper	Prof Zhang Guihong, Fudan University, China
Third Paper	Prof Srikant Kondapalli, JNU
Fourth Paper	Lt Gen (Army) Masahiro Kunimi (Retd), Okazaki Institute , Japan

Discussion

Session I: First Paper

Lieutenant General VR Raghavan, PVSM, USYSM, AVSM (Retd)

The rise to major power status of China has evoked great admiration. But it has also led to anxieties, not only amongst major powers, but also amongst its neighbours. One sees, in some ways, a long historical process in the rise of China. One well known historian had said, "By some natural law, in every Century there seems to emerge a country with power, the will and intellectual moral impetus to shape the international system according to its own values". He, for example, highlights that 17th Century was led by France under Richelieu, created the idea of nation state and national interest. We go on to 18th Century and see the Great Britain and the whole notion of balance of power, in 19th Century, Austria with Matternich and the idea of concert of nations, in 20th Century, indisputably the United States; which continues to influence international relations decisively and will continue to do so.

In the 21st Century, as the Keynote address indicated this morning, and this learned audience knows very well, the centre of gravity of global, geopolitical power is clearly shifting eastwards to Asia. China, Japan and India, and the economic power houses of East Asia, form the basis of this change. China remains undoubtedly the most powerful, in Asia. If we go by the four criteria, which experts apply to determine what makes a great power, the generally agreed four criteria are: Population and territory, resources (economic capability), political stability and military strength. By any of these criteria, China will rank as the top power in Asia and even outside Asia.

The recent economic global meltdown quite clearly shows that China has been more capable than major powers in managing such crises. To quote the US Treasury Secretary Geithner, "China has led the global economic recovery." At the last G 20 Summit, China's voice was the most powerful in critiquing the Western countries on their policy of profligate spending. China's unwillingness to regulate its currency to the global currencies, particularly to the Dollar, is a cause for economic discomfort, even as it demonstrates its capacity to chart its own course, disregarding others' needs.

Well informed and experienced as you are, you know of Chinese policy positions on major issues. How is the rapidly rising power going to be dealt with? How is it going to be engaged? How might India and China engage themselves with each other? Chinese policy trends can be seen through some major global positions which China has taken:-

(a) First is on the question of Taiwan, Tibet and Xingjian. Without placing a value judgment on the Chinese position, Chinese anxieties about what they call 'splittism' i.e. the centrifugal forces in China, is a major issue that everybody must bear in mind.

(b) There is a talk of 'string of pearls' – the Chinese bases in many places, seeking security of energy flows. You are all aware or what is otherwise called China's Malacca conundrum – the Malacca straits issue.

(c) Chinese muscular policies in South China Sea.

(d) Military and technology transfers of a sensitive nature, which have de-stabilised regions on its periphery.

(e) Economic assistance and aid, in return for energy supplies in Africa and other places. Recently, the Democratic Republic of Congo (DRC) has signed a massive contract for Chinese infrastructure in return for mineral supply. One Western paper called it, 'A Country on Sale'. The

IMF has cautioned the DRC that at this rate, their debt re-payment would become more difficult. That is the power of economic aid and grants which the Chinese are making. China's aid to states, clearly in violation of internationally accepted human rights standards, also disturbs many.

(f) There is a question of Chinese response to North Korea's nuclear ambitions and positions. While China is in the 6-Party talks with DPRK, its positions have been softer than the rest of the 5 members. Linked with this is the Chinese position on 'sanctions' against Iran for its nuclear transgressions. China has taken an independent line and has been against imposing sanctions.

(g) There is a question of China's military modernisation and capabilities in 'Space'.

On each of these issues a Chinese policy image can be built. The Chinese themselves, will have a finger to point at other countries.

Global power shifts have not occurred very frequently and rarely have they occurred peacefully. China's rise and the power shift, therefore, is watched very carefully. It produces extreme response from right wing to left wing. Let me give you two examples. In a survey conducted in Japan, between March and June this year, there were some conclusions. Initially, there were three perceptions in Japan, as given by that survey. First; that China behaves unpredictably. Second; its intentions are at best questionable. Third; the Japanese influence in China is very low. That is one perception. There is another perception from the USA of an extreme kind. On 25th March this year in the University of Chicago, the well known commentator Mearsheimer said, and I quote him, "There will be a Cold War between the USA and China. To stop China becoming the greatest power, the US will need to become allies with Japan, Russia, India, South Korea, Vietnam and Singapore, to form a balancing coalition around China."

Now this is another extreme of opinion. It just shows the anxieties that are created when a power shift is taking place.

Therefore, the question being asked today is: In 20 years time; around 2030, when China, if it maintains the current economic trend lines, will certainly overtake the US economy, what will be the position? What will be the status of internal stability in China? Will China be a cooperative and stabilising power? Or, will it be a threatening and de-stabilising power? As a result we see 'hedging strategies' by its neighbours and other powers, Japan's massive investments in China, and at the same time continuing to retain strong dependence on the USA, on security issues. Take for example Australia, with its massive increase in mineral exports to China which benefits the Australian economy, even as it forms part of a US led security alliance. Australia has made a strategic shift, from one of purely continental defence to an out of area capacity, and is building a new level of the Armed Forces. It was the Australians who talked of the proposal for a 'Strategic Quadrilateral' and the East Asian Summits etc. These are all responses to their anxieties on China.

How will the USA deal with China? Two approaches are under consideration. The first is of, 'Managed Great Power Relations'. In the year 2000, RAND Corporation produced a study done by Zalmay Khalilzad who later on became the Ambassador to Afghanistan etc. He looked at two options in that study, of 'containment' and 'engagement'. He recommended that the United States should follow a policy combining both containment and engagement. He called it 'Congagement', an interesting phrase! If we look at the manner in which the US Presidents have dealt with China from Mr Nixon to Clinton, to Mr Bush and now Mr Obama, the notion of managed great power relations can be seen to operate. We saw President George W Bush attempting a balancing role between Tokyo and Beijing. We saw the EU pushing sale of arms to China, against the US advice, because they knew that market was important to them.

How was this managed during the Cold War? Let me give you a quotation from Henry Kissinger's Memoirs. He talks of 'The Cold War Triangle' between the USA, Russia and China. I quote, "We had to walk a narrow path. We would make those agreements with the Soviet Union which we considered in our national interest. But we would give no assurance of a condominium, and we would resist any attempts by Moscow to achieve hegemony over China or elsewhere. We would keep China informed of our negotiations with the Soviet Union and in considerable detail, we would take account of Peking's views. We would conclude no agreement at the expense of Chinese interests but we would not give Peking veto over our actions. We followed this scrupulously – although since Moscow was the stronger party we briefed it much less precisely or frequently." How would the USA, which is now economically stressed, deal with a resurgent China? Allies are anxious and China's neighbours are watching. Both are coming to their own conclusions.

The second approach is of 'Strategic Assurance'. President Mr Obama has talked of no containment and not doing anything to harm China's interest. That policy has already come under severe criticism because it is feared by some that it will only re-inforce Chinese aggressive behaviour or assertive conduct. As the Keynote speaker mentioned and the Indian Prime Minister said in Washington, China's assertive behaviour disturbs India. Let me, therefore, read out what a US major newspaper, Washington Post, has said only last week, "Administrative officials seem to believe that the era of great-power competition is over. Unfortunately, that is not the reality in Asia. Contrary to optimistic predictions just a decade ago, China is behaving exactly as one would expect a great power to behave. As it has grown richer, China has used its wealth to build a stronger and more capable military. As its military power has grown, so have its ambitions. This is especially true of its naval ambitions. Not so long ago, our China experts believed it was absurd for China to aspire to a "blue-water" navy capable of operating far from its shores." The article goes on to quote the Secretary of Defence Robert Gates and the Pacific Area Commander Admiral Willard saying similar things.

Under the circumstances, what would Chinese and Indian reactions be in the years to come? There is a tug of war which we see reflected in the media etc. Both are jockeying for regional and global influence. Both are being sought as partners in the emerging security architecture. In my opinion the fears of a conflict between China and India are overstated. Both, despite many disagreements, have joint interests and are joined in their commitments. They have shared commitments, for example, on 'No First Use' of nuclear weapons. They are committed not to test nuclear weapons. They both await the US to ratify the CTBT before they will think of joining it. Both have combined joint naval and military exercises. They share views on climate change and emissions policy.

It is useful to note a World Bank Report of 2007, titled, 'Dancing with the Giants: China, India and the Global Economy'. The Report "The rise of China and India as major trading nations in manufacturing and services will affect world markets, systems....substantially, and hence change the environment in which other countries make their economic decisions." This has already begun to happen.

China's rise to great power position is not in doubt. The approaches its neighbours and great powers adopt to meet the 'Rise of China', with the two options that I have indicated, will determine not only their relations with China, but the strategic balance in this Century.

Session I: Second Paper

Professor Zhang Guihong

During my presentation, I will all answer the four questions listed in Session 1 agenda, one by one. First question is: *'What is China's grand strategy?'* China's grand strategy can be summarised, 'As peaceful development for or towards harmonious world, which highlights the connection between domestic development and foreign relations'. In early 1980's, China's leader Deng Xio Ping put up the concept of 'peace and development'. Since 2003, China's new leadership, Hu-Jintao and Weng-Jiabao have proposed several new concepts, such as; peaceful rise, peaceful development and harmonious world. After lot of comments, evaluation and debate in Academia and the Government, these concepts have been guidelines of the Chinese foreign policy in the new Century. I integrate these three concepts in one phrase, 'peaceful development for harmonious world.' Here, 'peaceful development' is the means and the road to achieve the goal and ideal of a 'harmonious world'. This grand strategy is deeply rooted in Chinese cultural tradition, socio economic situation and international environment. Here, I would like to evaluate the main features and dimensions of this grand strategy.

(a) First is the domestic situation as the background, and then comes international environment. After nearly 30 years of economic reform and opening up, China's new leadership believes that China should have a balanced, scientific and sustainable development model. Current GDP, environment friendly development and people first policy etc; this new understanding and thinking about development is termed Beijing 'consensus'. Internationally, the new Chinese leadership sees 'peace and development' as the new theme of the era. To put forward a series of new concepts, such as 'new security concept'. We mean three things: common development, international responsibility, harmonious region etc. The new strategy is focussing on multilateralism, consultation and democratisation.

(b) Second point is about the aims and the means of this grand strategy. The goal of the grand strategy is not only to maintain national security and integrity or sovereignty, but it is also to construct a favourable and stable national environment for economic development. Stability of the surrounding area and international system is crucial to achieve this goal. With regard to the means, the Government has attached more importance to economy, energy, public diplomacy, multilateral approach and mutually beneficial cooperation.

(c) Third point concerns intention and capability of the grand strategy. According to this new grand strategy, China is more likely than before to take initiative and make use of its growing economic capabilities, to construct preferred international environment rathar than merely adapting itself to it. China's new leadership has more confidence to express Chinese interests and concerns and actively make proposals and suggestions for international affairs. As you can see, everytime Chinese top leaders visit foreign countries to address international conferences, they respond and make some proposals on international affairs. As interest and influence expands worldwide, China today is emphasising more on international contribution and responsibility, e.g., in the field of UN Peacekeeping operations and assistance to African countries.

The second question is: *'Is China's political system compatible with uninterrupted economic growth?'* China's 'one ruling party' system has inherent advantage as well as disadvantage in promoting economic growth. The advantages are: the ability of social mobilisation, continuum of the government and its policy, political stability and administrative efficiency etc. On the other hand, the disadvantages include: lack of transparency and freedom, weaker civil society, serious corruption, high administrative costs. China today confronts a lot of problems and challenges including rising unemployment, latent official corruption, weak legal system, growing regional disparity, increasing gap between the rich and the poor and unequal access to education, population problem, religious bottlenecks and severe environment problems. All these problems can only be resolved through deepening of reforms for the proposed building of market economy and a 'rule of law' of state.

The third question: *'Is China's rise peaceful?'* Yes, from my understanding. There are always doubts challenging China's peaceful rise. Some argue that the concept of peaceful rise is unlikely; because so far in world history, there has never been any power that has risen peacefully. According to international theory, peace is not maintained just by your own will. It is a business involving at least two actors. Others think that given the values and origins of the political system, China's successful rise may not be acceptable to some countries, particularly for the USA. They are also suspicious about China's commitment to peaceful development and environment of the world. They think, that the key programme is about how the Chinese leaders and people will deal with this issue, 20 years later. Others believe that China's strong quest for energy and resources may come in conflict with national interests of some countries. However, I hold an optimistic view on the prospects of China's rise which is based on the following reasons:-

(a) Looking back sixty years, when China was weak and poor from 1949 to 1979, it was involved in military conflicts and wars with the USA, Soviet Union, India and Vietnam. When China became strong and a leader since 1980, things have changed.

(b) Peaceful and stable foreign relations, otherwise the result will be a losing game instead of a win-win situation.

(c) China has benefitted from the current international system. Though there are some unfair and unequal characterstics of the current international system, China believes that it can be improved gradually through reforms. So, China prefers to promote innovation of international system in a cooperative way rather than to be a revolutionary.

(d) As the USA has declined relatively, it cannot easily use force as a confrontational means, to either contain China or to prevent its rise. President Obama said ten days ago in Tokyo, that the US will not seek to contain China. According to the US-China joint statement issued in Beijing a week ago, the US reiterated that, it welcomed a strong, prosperous and successful China that played a greater role in international affairs. China welcomes the USA and Asia Pacific nations that contribute to peace, stability and prosperity in the region. Both sides reiterated that they were committed to building a positive, cooperative and comprehensive US-China relationship for the 21st Century. The two countries will take concrete actions to steadily build a partnership to address common challenges.

(e) Europe, Russia and some other major powers make positive comments on China's demonstration of peaceful rise and I hope, our Indian friends will have similar and more positive attitude on China's rise after this Conference.

The last question: *'What are China's politico-diplomatic moves in support of her Grand strategy'?* According to my understanding, the considered view in China is that there are four dimensions or features of foreign policy which form the framework of political-diplomatic moves in support of her grand strategy. They are :-

(a) The first dimension is: China regards its relationship with its neighbouring countries as a priority. So, the first feature is to try and establish a good neighbourhood over land and sea in the neighbouring countries.

(b) The second dimension is: China regards being largest developing country as the basis of their foreign policy. China tries to stand up with and support the developing countries.

(c) The third dimension is: China regards its relations with major powers including the USA, Russia, European Union and India as a key to its foreign policy. China tries to build up different kinds of partnerships with these major powers.

(d) The fourth dimension is: The international arena where China sees space for itself, where it can contribute by playing a greater role. China seeks to actively participate and make its contribution. These actions form the approach of its political-diplomatic moves, including several other points, e.g. settling border issues with neighbouring countries through negotiations. As you can see that we have solved border problems with Russia and Myanmar. Second is to increase economic relations independently with countries in the region. China has been deeply involved in regional integration in the South East Asia and the Central Asia and tries to act in cooperation with South Asian countries to promote prosperity in the region.

(e) The last point is, to become a more active member of the global and regional institutions.

Session I : Third Paper

Professor Srikanth Kondapalli

Abstract

While China had not issued an explicit grand strategic outline of its current and future course of action domestically and internationally, several recent pronouncements by the Chinese leadership and other stakeholders indicate that certain interpretations could be made of these statements. Initially, as the Common Programme of September 1949 and subsequently the four constitutions (till 1982 and since amended) indicated China's objectives domestically are to enhance substantially GDP figures. In the early 1980s, Deng Xiaoping emphasised on "economic development at the centre" and advocated "hiding capabilities and biding for time". As the 16th Chinese Communist Party Congress in 2002 and reiterated by the 17th Party Congress in 2007, further emphasised, China's goal is to build a "well-off society" by 2020 – that of reaching the socio-economic standards of the developed Western European countries. All these are to convert the nation into a "rich country and strong army". Internationally, China had emphasised, for a long time in the past, on minimalist foreign policy goals of stressing and protecting its perceived sovereignty and territorial integrity and maintaining its perspective. However, as a consequence of the rise of China in hard and soft power aspects, new approaches are noticed in China's external responses that point towards maximalist perspectives, viz., active role in international political and economic institutions, "Beijing Consensus", G-2, etc. It is argued in this paper that although China's sights are now set at the strategic levels and it has been concertedly preparing for the realisation of "strategic opportunities", its ability to realise these goals are likely to be challenged by rising countries in the region, in addition to the US.

Introduction

While China had not issued any explicit grand strategic outline of its current and future course of action domestically and internationally, several recent pronouncements by the Chinese leadership and other stakeholders indicate that certain interpretations could be made of these statements. Initially, as the Common Programme of September 1949 and subsequently the four constitutions (till 1982, and since amended) indicated China's objectives domestically are to consolidate the Communist Party's rule in the country and enhance substantially GDP figures. Although this blueprint had substantially altered – given the political movements related to Great Leap Forward and the Cultural Revolution - a common thread among these "two line" struggles indicated to the relevance, nay centrality, of the Communist Party's rule as well as the necessity for furthering the agricultural and industrial output, while at the same time protecting perceived claims on Tibet, Xinjiang, Inner Mongolia, Taiwan, Hong Kong and Macau issues.

In the early 1980s, Deng Xiaoping emphasised on "economic development at the centre" and advocated "hiding capabilities and biding for time". Several Chinese premiers and presidents had mentioned that the GDP figures would be quadrupled. As President Hu Jintao mentioned in his address to the Bo Ao Forum for Asia in April 2004, the Chinese government intends to "quadruple the 2000 GDP to 4 trillion US dollars with a per capita GDP of 3,000 US dollars".[1] As the 16th Chinese Communist Party (CCP) Congress in 2002 and reiterated by the 17th Party Congress in 2007, further emphasised, China's goal is to build a "well-off society" by 2020 – that of reaching the socio-economic standards of the developed Western European countries. All these are to convert the nation into a "rich country and a strong army". [2] To some extent these were met – not only were Hong Kong and Macau united under China in 1997 and 1999 respectively, but also that the GDP had been increased to an estimated $4.6 trillion in 2009– making China as the third largest economy after the United States and Japan. Next year, it is estimated that China would be able to displace Japan in these economic figures. Chinese government statistics indicated that, despite the global financial meltdown in 2008-09, China in 2009 was able to maintain 8.7 per cent economic growth rate and exported $2 trillion worth of goods (while Germany exported $1.17 trillion). Also, surging exports contributed to the enhancement in the coffers of China – estimated at more than $2.2 trillion by 2009. Militarily as well, China made significant progress and with the $70 billion in official defence budget in 2009, it becomes the largest spender in Asia.

Internationally, China had emphasised, for a long time in the past, on minimalist foreign policy goals of stressing and protecting its perceived sovereignty and territorial integrity and maintaining its perspective. As a consequence, it was only after Taiwan was displaced from the United Nations in 1971 that the People's Republic of China (PRC) was able to take its 'rightful' place at this international forum with veto power. Considerable diplomatic pressure was mounted on Hong Kong, Macau, Tibet, Xinjiang and Inner Mongolian issues as well. Also, foreign policy was made to serve the national strategy of economic development – by attracting foreign direct investment, technology and sustaining exports. However, as a consequence of the rise of China in hard and soft power aspects, new approaches are noticed in China's external responses that point towards moving into maximalist foreign policy perspectives, viz., active role in international political and economic institutions, 'Beijing Consensus', G-2, etc. These provide scope for the flowering of more articulate China's grand strategy formulations in the future.

This paper analyses the main strands in the Chinese debates on China's grand strategy, its rise in the recent two decades, and argues that although China's sights are now set at the strategic levels and it has been concertedly preparing for the realisation of 'strategic opportunities', its ability to realise these goals are likely to be challenged by rising countries in the region, in addition to the US. Nevertheless, a few caveats are in order. While the concept of grand strategy originated in the US[3], and while very few Chinese historically delved on such subjects with the exception of some Chinese scholars in the last decade, a few Chinese concepts come closer to this phenomenon, viz., "grand strategy" (*da zhanlue*), great power diplomacy (*daguo waijiao*), strategy (*zhanlue*), etc.[4] Secondly, it appears that the Chinese discourse on the subject has similar themes as in the western literature, although several Chinese still consider that they have to further develop the theoretical contours of such a phenomenon.[5] In this sense, as a developing country, China is yet to unveil full-fledged and comprehensive grand strategic formulations and can be said that this is still in the making.[6]

China's Grand Strategy

As a country which insists on learning from the ancient strategies, China is legion in attracting global attention in terms of grand strategy, although as a relatively developing country in the recent period, it is still in the process of unveiling major aspects of such a strategy.[7] In the pre-modern and modern periods, several Chinese have indicated to their interest in grand strategy, although largely not cohesive and 'grand' in scale. Thus, Sun Zi in the sixth century BC is credited to have triggered the Chinese minds on overcoming the adversaries through strategy and without using force. Wei Yuan, in the light of the battering with which China was subjected by the Western powers during the late Qing dynasty period, had proposed principles for the rejuvenation of the country. The Hundred Days of reform of 1898 proved to be inconclusive in the fast changing fortunes of the empire. Likewise, the May Fourth Movement, which galvanised several sections of the population, proved inconclusive. Dr Sun Yat-sen, considered by both CCP and the Kuomintang (KMT) as their founding father, proposed 'Three Principles of People's Livelihood' (with nationalism, democracy and livelihood), which appeared comprehensive solutions for those times. Subsequently, the country became a victim of the Japanese inroads and civil war, which forbid any grand strategy formulations. After the People's Republic of China (PRC) was established in October 1949, conditions were conducive for such strategies, although the country was soon drawn into wars with the US in the Korean Peninsula (1951-53), with India (1962), the then Soviet Union (1969) and with Vietnam (1979), even as intermittent skirmishes with Taiwan confined China to the East Asia box.

Mao Zedong, Zhou Enlai and others did provide for strategic thinking and inputs between 1949-76 as reflected in the 'leaning to one side' (towards the then Soviet Union), Five Principles for Peaceful Co-existence or 'good neighbourliness' policy and Three World construct. Yet, the weak material base for such grand design proved costly for China till Deng Xiaoping's reform and opening up provided for certain concrete inputs such as is reflected in the concept of 'taoguang yanghui' (hiding capabilities and biding for time/maintaining a low profile). Essentially, this slogan, unveiled in 1989, called for focussing on economic development, engaging all countries for the smooth flow of investments and technologies into China and even postponing conflicts for a long time except, on core sovereignty issues.

In the last three decades of reform and opening up, China also debated the grand strategic contours. Essentially including the minimalist foreign policy positions of Mao and others (viz., the core interests - sovereignty over Taiwan, Hong Kong, Macao and 'lost territories'), Deng's China (inclusive of Jiang Zemin from 1989-2004 and currently under Hu Jintao), emboldened, as it were, with the increases in comprehensive national power of the country, unveiled a grand strategy.[8] Although still in the making, such a vision envisaged firstly enhancing the material wealth of the country – with economic development at the centre and under the CCP's rule. Disintegration of the Soviet Union that reduced military threats from the North, favourable reform policies, engagement with the outside world, multilateral efforts with several 'partners' globally and changes in the CCP policies[9] - all provided for inputs into the Chinese grand strategy and implementation.[10] Indeed, China had unveiled – with relative successes – several concepts and initiated steps in this regard.[11] Mention should be made of the occupation of the Paracels from Vietnam in 1974, Mischief

Reef from the Philippines in 1988, expansion in the exclusive economic zone in 1992, commons security concept, new security concept, and multilateral initiatives in the political and security fields (such as with Shanghai Cooperation Organisation and East Asian Summit) and in the economic fields (Bo Ao Forum), conducted grand events such as Beijing Olympics in August 2008[12], etc.

To summarise and outline the major components of China's grand strategy, in brief, the Chinese leadership believes in enhancing firstly its economic and military profile in the international system so as to form the foundation for its concerted role in the international order. Three concepts recur in the Chinese debates, viz., international system, international pattern and the international order. While the first two indicate to an objective situation of interactions between states (and also non-state actors), the third concept - order – indicates to the subjective desires of the country concerned. In China's case, as reflected in the six white paper issued on national defence and the 16th and 17th Party Congresses reports[13], it can be argued that China presently wants to maintain and support the current international strategic situation so as to build a "well-off society" by 2020. At the same time, it wants to retain its autonomy in the international relations and even become a great power, specifically in the light of the decline of the US in events such as Iraq and Afghanistan.[14] China's premier Wen Jiabao, at the dinner meeting with the US President during the latter's visit to Beijing in November 2009, also rejected the idea of G-2.

China Rise Phenomenon

The above grand formulations have to be fulfilled by the comprehensive rise of China. The phenomenon of China rise is of recent origin, although some Chinese trace back such rise to the halcyon days of the Middle Kingdom. Nevertheless, it includes enhancements in the comprehensive national power of the country, specifically in the last decade of Chinese economic, military and soft power increase.[15] Several Chinese scholars debated the phenomenon and strategies for China's rise in the last decade. Enlisted below are some main ideas in China.

The concept of 'peaceful rise' (*heping jueqi*) of China was proposed by Zheng Bijian, vice president of the CCP Central Party School at Bo Ao Forum for Asia in 2003. However, a year before this speech, nearly twenty Chinese scholars reportedly had worked out the major arguments of this thesis to systematically counter the security concerns expressed by China's neighbours and those in the West.[16] Zheng Bijian in his speech at the BoAo Forum of Asia on 25 April 2004 observed candidly that China's rise may usher competition in the Asia-Pacific region, but argued that such competition would take the path of "friendship, cooperation, mutual benefit and win-win situation, not competition of arms buildup, or competition for spheres of influence or hegemony". He also advocated establishing "communities of common interests" in East Asia and "sub-regional mechanisms with different functions and features, and conduct flexible cooperation to achieve marked results". Subsequently, as the following section indicates, several officials and scholars in China have reflected on this phenomenon. However, to ward off any negative connotations that 'rise' indicates; in the discourse of late has been a tendency to rephrase the phenomenon as merely 'peace and development'.

A comprehensive description of China rise is provided by Men Honghua, an associate professor at the international strategic research institute of the Chinese Communist Party (CCP) Central Committee Party School. Men argued that in explaining the complex phenomenon of China rise, scholars and others in China and elsewhere have proposed different theories as follows:

(a) *'Zhongguo jiyu lun'* (Theory of China as a favourable opportunity);

(b) *'Zhongguo gongxian lun'* (Theory of China contribution);

(c) *'Zhongguo weixie lun'* (China threat theory);

(d) 'Zhongguo bengkui lun' (China collapse theory); and

(e) 'Zhongguo jingji shuifen lun' (China's economic moisture (surplus exaggeration) theory).[17]

Each one of these theories, as is evident, in one way or the other have shaped our understanding about the phenomenal changes that China is undergoing not only in its domestic political, economic and military sectors but also in its interactions with other countries at the regional and global levels.

Ren Donglai traced the earliest work in China on peaceful rise phenomenon to Yan Xuetong who wrote an article *'Lengzhan hou Zhongguo de duiwai anquan zhanlue'* (China's external security strategy in the post Cold War era) in the 8th issue of China Institute of Contemporary International Relations journal in 1995. Yan discussed three main aspects of China's cultural tradition, national interests and strategic calculations. More pronounced on the subject were the views of Yan in his 1997 co-edited publication on *'Zhongguo Jueqi: Guoji huanqing pinggu'* [China Rise: International Environmental Assessment] (Tianjin People's Publications, 1997). The concept had emerged in the light of 'China threat theory'. Yan defined 'rise' as the gap between the burgeoning strength of a large country and the simultaneous reduction of other powerful nations or even surpassing the strength of these latter powerful countries. So the crucial words here are 'catching up and surpassing' and 'acceleration' in the power of the rising country.[18]

Yan Xuetong identified three main streams of thought in China and elsewhere on this subject:

(a) 'Zhongguo weixie lun' [China threat theory] by scholars, mainly outside China

(b) 'Dache lilun' [Hitchhike theory] by mainly Chinese scholars who argued that since rising Germany and Japan failed quickly, it is better

for China to follow the path of avoiding opposition to the US hegemony.

(c) 'Shidai butong lun' [Distinct era theory] by 'objective' scholars who viewed that in the current period, China should follow a policy of 'good neighbourliness' and blend with the international system and avoid using military force.

(d) 'Xin renshi lun' [New understanding theory] sported mainly by those closer to the Chinese government who viewed current Chinese policy as 'economic construction at centre' and that China will not contend for hegemony with the US. It rules out use of force. Famous exponent of this school is Zheng Bijian when he made a speech at Bo Ao Forum in 2003.[19]

A Chinese writer mentioned that under this concept China would strive for international peace and all-round development of the country. According to Zheng, 'peaceful rise' would be the national strategic principle in which there are three sub clauses, as follows:

(a) Push forward with determination the path of socialist market economy with Chinese characteristics and socialist political and economic democratic system

(b) Promoting Chinese civilisational aspects, and

(c) Pursue overall regional, economic and social development and harmonious growth of urban and countryside for building a well-off society.[20]

While some scholars have pointed out that the current "rise" of China is its fourth such rise in its history, most of the accounts generally trace to the last two decades. Nevertheless, the following two scholars' assessments are based on historical explanations, while the rest focus on contemporary events. A revisionist analysis of historical events of the last 5,000 years revealed to Xu Boyuan not an expansionistic empire from the two main

Yellow and Yangtze river valley civilisations but that of cultural stability. Xu argued that in an age of globalisation, cultural stability of the country would be an asset.[21] Stating that of the 28 civilisations, 18 have disappeared from earth, Zhou Bajun argued that 21st Century belongs to that of China. Given the economic dynamism of the Asia-Pacific region, especially in China, Hong Kong, Macao and Taiwan, this region is poised to become the focus of the world.[22]

After following the debates within China and other countries, several interesting themes were outlined by Dai Wenming and others in describing the China rise phenomenon. Does the rise of China entail any negative impact on others as mentioned in the 'China threat' theory? Is there a specific 'China experience' that can be learnt or emulated by others, specifically in the economic growth rates? Is there any specific 'Chinese contribution' or 'China opportunity'? Given the official rhetoric about China being a responsible country, would this lead to a 'strong China that does not determine'? They bring about issues related to the 'overheating' of the economy, economic restructuring, population ageing, critical energy and environmental security aspects, and the like. They conclude, with observations from scholars at Shanghai, that China has participated in multilateral institutions, respected the United Nations mandates, entered the World Trade Organisation, etc and these reflect its responsible behaviour.[23]

Luo Yuan, chairman of Strategy Research Institute of the PLA Academy of Military Science, argued that China's rise would result in national cohesion and would make the country most powerful in the Asia-Pacific region. He proposed three stages in such a rise:

(a) Construction [yingzao] stage in which China should promote peaceful environment in its periphery and safeguard national sovereignty and territorial integrity

(b) Moulding [suzao] stage in which China would pursue policies to shape the events and regain lost territories

(c) Plan and control [*jinglue*] stage in which by political [or military ?] means the international community accepts China's efforts in building a new political economic international order that ensures strategic balance and stability.

Luo stated that of all these three stages, currently China is at the first stage mentioned above. He contended that emphasis on peace does not mean that China should neglect the defence sector. Indeed it should strengthen its defence forces. In his support, Luo cites an old proverb "*youguo wufang, guojiang buguo*" [a country without defence would not remain a country]. On the other hand, even if China rises without any military backing, it would not be able to retain its influence long and will certainly decline. The experience of Qing Dynasty clearly validates this assertion, according to Luo. Therefore, for a rising China, the military should have to provide 'escort' functions. Indeed, the only existing powerful countries in the world are those with strong military strength. Luo advocates that higher attention should be paid to the defence sector during the course of China's rise. This is conducive for China to achieve higher strategic ability to not only wage a dozen local wars successfully but, more importantly, restrain a war from breaking. The second aspect that China can possess, by emphasising military modernisation, is strategic autonomy that ensures independence from adversary's control of strategic resources. The third aspect that Luo bestows on China, on the path to rapid rise with defence preparation, is its strong international coordinating [*xietiao*] ability. Luo warns, China if it neglects/forgets war preparation, it would face disaster in its path to peaceful rise [*heping jueqi, wangzhan biwei*].[24]

For China's rise in the next 30-50 years, it should abide by the rules of the global order and UN resolutions, achieve internal stability and avoid Tiananmen Square kind of incidents and resolve internal socio-economic problems like river-water diversion, grain production, urban migration, etc.

Li Zizheng here implies that China and India, which have huge potential, should learn from the lessons of the US unilateral actions.[25]

According to Professor Gu Haibing of the People's University, China needs to adopt a great power strategy for the coming years as the international influence of China is set to grow phenomenally. He argues that keeping in view China's large territory, resources, faster economic growth rates, the number of millionaires in the country, living standards, and increase in its strength, China needs to follow its own 'survival' strategy. While a small power would adopt a strategy of allying with other powers for its security, China, being a large power, should adopt a great power strategy in which there should be a coordination between the concepts of strong/powerful nation (*qiangguo*), rich people (*fumin*) and environment (*huanqing meijing*). Most important, according to Gu, is the emphasis placed on *qiangguo* (powerful nation) than to the other elements. Therefore, China should choose this as the 'fulcrum' of all its strategies and enhance the military capabilities of the country to ensure the country's 'independence'. He does agree that there exists antagonistic contradiction between the co-existence of a strong nation and rich people or environmental problems as a result of building up of a powerful nation, but argues that unity between the two can be arrived at through proper coordination. Gu notes that China's rise faces stiff competition [*qiangli jingzheng*] from India and from the resourceful Japan.[26]

Conclusion

China's comprehensive rise in the global power matrix had kindled debates on China's grand strategy in the recent period. For the first time in its history, China is being counted internationally due to its rise in CNP terms – it is respected or feared – a prophesy Napoleon spoke about in the 19th century. As China entered into globalisation phase, international security and strategic contours are increasingly getting enmeshed with China as a major factor. However, there are several fault lines in the linear progress of China's

CNP, viz., CCP stability, widening ethnic tensions, growing income inequalities and popular unrest, growing middle-class aspirations, environmental degradation, and dependency on high-seas and trans-boundary regions for trade and energy supplies. Nevertheless, the Chinese leadership had taken some corrective measures to wriggle out of these challenges. For instance, efforts are being made to broad-base the 73 million-cadre CCP. Private entrepreneurs are now being admitted into the party and the relevant constitutional provisions are being amended. Secondly, to counter the three evils (separatism, extremism and splittism), para-military forces are being strengthened and counter-terrorism exercises launched with concerned countries. Thirdly, China is also taking initiatives in projecting power as reflected in the peace-keeping operations abroad, counter-piracy operations off the coast of Somalia, and naval and air force build-up. Yet, the guidelines of Deng Xiaoping on biding for time and regional security dynamics could challenge the balance - thus posing concerns for China's rise in the long-term perspective. China's stance on Indian border areas, and on Japan and Vietnam is instructive in this regard.

End Notes

1 See for the full text of Hu Jintao's speech on April 24, 2004 at <http:// www.boaoforum.org/boao/2004nh/cd/t20040424_733981.shtml> accessed on December 20, 2004

2 For an extensive discussion on this topic see Hu Angang ed. *Zhongguo Da Zhanlue* (China's Grand Strategy) (Hangzhou: Zhejiang People's Publications, 2002) pp. 3-37

3 See Paul Kennedy (ed.), **Grand Strategies in War and Peace** (New Haven: Yale University Press, 1991)

4 See, for instance, Xiao Jialing and Tang Xianxing eds. *Daguo Waijiao: Lilun, juece,tiaozhan* (Great Power Diplomacy: Theory, decision-making and challenge) (Shishi Publications, Shanghai, 2003) 2 volumes; Hu Angang ed. *Zhongguo Da Zhanlue* (China's

Grand Strategy) (Hangzhou: Zhejiang People's Publications, 2002) and Shi Yinhong, *Zhanlue Wenti Sanshi Bain – Zhongguo Duiwai Zhanlue Sikao* (Thirty Studies on Strategy – Reflections on the External Strategic of China) (Beijing: People's University Publications, 2008)

5Avery Goldstein had argued that such a grand strategy started emerging in the Chinese thinking from 1996 after several ad hoc measures before by the leadership. See "The Diplomatic Face of China's Grand Strategy: A Rising Power's Emerging Choice" *The China Quarterly (*2001) pp.835-64

6According to David Finkelstein, crucial to understanding the subject are a few fundamentals, viz., well defined objectives; development of concepts, approaches and concrete policies to achieve these objectives; development of capacities for implementation; coordination and adjustment. See his "Commentary on China's External Grand Strategy" *38th Taiwan-U.S. Conference on Contemporary China*, The Brookings Institution & National Chengchi University, July 14-15, 2009

7 See Michael D. Swaine and Ashley J. Tellis, *Interpreting China's Grand Strategy: Past, Present, and Future* (Santa Monica, CA: RAND, 2000)

8 See Di Dongsheng, "Continuities and Changes: A Comparative Study on China's New Grand Strategy" *Historia Actual Online* No.12 (2007), pp. 7-18 and Chen Mumin, "Going Global: The Chinese Elite's Views of Security Strategy in the 1990s " *Asian Perspective* vol. 29 no. 2 pp. (2005) 133-77

9These latter included Deng Xiaoping's Four Cardinal Principles of making the CCP as the focus; Jiang Zemin's ideas on "three represents" to broad base the CCP; and currently Hu Jintao's "harmonious world" to reduce tensions domestically and internationally.

10Liselotte Odgaard had argued that in the post-Cold War period, China, taking a cue from Matternich's grand strategy, is struggling with the outside world in order to avoid being labelled as a secondary power in the international order. See "Metternich and China's Post-Cold War Grand strategy" Institute for Strategy, Faculty of Strategy and Military Operations, Royal Danish Defence College, Copenhagen, 2009

11 See Philip C. Saunders, "China's Global Activism: Strategy, Drivers, and Tools" Institute for National Strategic Studies, US NDU Occasional Paper 4 October 2006

12 On this aspect and how Olympics contributed to enhancing China's public diplomacy, see Qiu Huafei, " Public Diplomacy: China's Grand Foreign Strategy" *PD Case Study: Beijing Olympics* (Issue 1 Winter 2009) at <www.publicdiplomacy magazine.org>

13 See for the six white papers at <http://www.china.org.cn> or <http://english.chinamil.com.cn> See also the US Department of Defense papers on the military power of China at <http://www.dod.gov>

14 See Wang Yuan-Kang, "China's Grand Strategy and US Primacy: Is China balancing American power?" *The Brooking Institution* July 2006

15 See Michael E. Brown, Owen R. Cote, Jr., Sean M. Lynn-Jones and Steven E. Miller (eds.), *The Rise of China* (Cambridge, MA: MIT Press, 2000); and Ahn Byung-Joon, "The Rise of China and the Future of East Asian Integration" *Asia-Pacific Review* vol. 11 no. 2 (2004) pp. 18-35

16 For an excellent analysis, see Ting Yong-Kang, "'Peaceful Ascendancy' and Cross-Straits Relations" at <http://www.peaceforum.org.tw> accessed on January 4, 2005

17 Men Honghua, "*Zhongguo heping jueqi de guoji zhanlue kuangjia*" (International strategic framework of China's peaceful rise) *Shijie Jingji yu Zhengzhi (World Economy & Politics)* (Beijing) No. 6 (2004). The "China threat theory" reflects to the concerns expressed by scholars outside China on the concerted military modernisation programme, specifically in the military doctrinal changes towards offensive orientations (like the PLA's debates on "pre-emptive strike strategy" (*xianfa zhiren*)), emphasis placed on navy, air force, rapid response forces and strategic rocket forces and to the lack of transparency in the military fields, especially in the defence budget. The "China collapse theory" is traced to Gordon Chang's work, *The Coming Collapse of China* (New York: Random House, 2001).

18 Ren Donglai, "*Daguo jueqi de zhidu guangjia he sixiang chuantong*" (The system frame and ideological tradition of Great Power rise) *Zhongguo Zhengzhi Xue* May 12,

2004 (originally published in Shanghai Academy of Social Science publication *"Cong Lishi Jiaodu kan Daguo jueqi: Bijiao yu Jiejian" (Looking from the view point of Great Power Rise: Comparisons and Lessons Drawn)* Wujiang, Jiangsu Province, March 2004). (All references to Zhongguo Zhengzhi Xue are at <http://www.cpd.org.cn> accessed on July 23, 2005). Ren noted, citing Mandelbaum's thesis, that a country can decisively march to become a power in the international field when, in the process of rising, defeats another major power through military means.

19 Yan Xuetong, *"Heping jueqi yu baozhang heping- Jianlun Zhongguo jueqi de zhanlue yu celue"* (Peaceful rise and safeguarding peace- A brief theoretical note on the strategy and policy of China rise) *Guoji Wenti Yanjiu* (Studies on International Issues) No. 3 (2004)

20 Zheng Bijian cited at *"'Zhongguo heping jueqi' lun youlai"* (Origins of the theory of 'China's peaceful rise'" *Zhongguo Zhengzhi Xue* May 18, 2004 (originally published in *Guoji Xianqu Daobao*). Zheng insisted here that China should follow a foreign policy of peace and development in which it would not bully or exploit other countries, in addition to formulating a new security concept that stresses mutual security and mutual benefit to all concerned.

21 Xu Boyuan, *"Zhongguo heping jueqi de lishi yiju"* (The historical essence of China's peaceful rise) *Zhongguo Zhengzhi Xue* May 27, 2004

22 Zhou Bajun, *"'Zhongguo jueqi' yiwei shenme?"* (What is the meaning of 'China rise'?) *Zhongguo Zhengzhi Xue (Chinese Political Studies)* May 26, 2005 (originally printed in *Hong Kong Business Daily*). Zhou traced Chinese strength in terms of rise in Gross Domestic Product figures after the reform and opening policies were launched in 1978.

23 Dai Wenming, *et.al.* *"Zhongguo de weilai xingxiang: Fennu de minzu haishi lixing de daguo?"* (The future image of China: Angry nation or a rational great power?) *Zhongguo Zhengzhi Xue (Chinese Political Studies)* September 14, 2004

24 See for the views of several Chinese scholars cited above, Tao Deyan and Zhang Binyang, *"Zhuanjia zonglun Zhongguo heping jueqi jinglue"* *Zhongguo Zhengzhi Xue* May 18, 2004 (originally published in *Guoji Xianqu Daobao*)

25 Li Zizheng cited at "*Jueqi de Zhongguo ying geng lijie shijie xianghu yicun zhongyao xing*" (Rising China should understand the significance of mutual global co-existence) *Zhongguo Zhengzhi Xue* June 22, 2004

26 "*Zhongguo ying xuanze daguo zhanlue: Fang Zhongguo Renmin daxue jiashou Gu Haibing*" (China needs to adopt a great power strategy: Interview with Chinese People's University professor Gu Haibing) *Zhongguo Zhengzhi Xue* June 29, 2004 (article originally published in *China Economic Times)*

Session I : Fourth Paper

Lieutenant General Masahiro Kunimi (Retd)

My presentation will address the same questions from a different point of view.

What is China's grand strategy?

China is parading the national slogan of "A great resurgence of the Chinese race, since the Chinese Revolution of 1911". It may not be clear what is meant by "the great resurgence of the Chinese race", but observing the GDP of the world's nations in 1820, it is said that China held the first rank with 28.7 per cent, India the second with 16 per cent, France the third with 5.4 per cent, and the USA the fourth with 1.8 per cent. China seems to be aiming at a second advent of that position.

At the end of 1970's, it took one important decision about reformation and liberation policy. By holding fast to a ruling system by the Communist Party, and through reformation and liberation policies, China now seeks an identity as "a rich and powerful nation," or, to use a different term, to become, both, an economic and a military power. After 30 years, China still continues this policy.

On 1 October, 2009, the Chinese showed their power plus their political system. It had been predicted that China would be accomplishing social change because of it's economic growth and progress in modernisation, would pursue capitalism, democracy, and peace. However, the achievement of economic development in China does not directly lead to political reforms of the Chinese Communist Party. Even within the Party there is strong resistance to political reforms. However, while China becomes strong and affluent, the dictatorial inclination of the Communist Party is becoming pronounced – which strengthens its challenging posture as a new power in the leadership of Asia.

Peaceful rise or not, China continues to pursue economic growth for future development through reforms and liberation policies. In order to sustain its economic development and domestic stability, China tries to ward off regional destabilisation. It is essential for China to secure resources such as petroleum and iron ore that underpin economic growth. To maintain resources, China is deepening relations with non-democratic and anti-USA countries, and against such countries that compete with China in the race to secure resources. The likelihood of China being vigorously antagonistic is quite high. To maintain domestic stability, China would cut off trade with countries that criticise the policy of Chinese Communist Party.

In the interests of rising China, the Chinese Communist Party is to formulate individual, logical self-justifying policies, and to resolutely put even belligerent policies into practice in order to gain victory over competing nations. However, China avoids decisive confrontation with great powers such as the USA and Russia. This point is very important because China started Vietnamese war first, because at that time China wanted to teach Vietnam a lesson. Now, how does China have a right to give a lesson to Vietnam is asked by the United Nation's General Assembly? Will only the Chinese Communist Party decide so or not? The NATO countries also want to know it. This is very important.

What are China's politico-diplomatic moves in support of its grand strategy?

The basis of diplomatic strategy is omni directional partnership to serve "economic interests." China aims at "multipolarisation" and economic "globalisation" in the future as distinctive from the "bipolar structure" of the Cold War era and the "uni-polar, multi-power" structure of the post Cold War period. At the collapse of the former Soviet Union, no country could directly point out to the USA. China wants to be similar in form to that of former Soviet Union, directly pointing to the USA and irritating the US superpower. China takes a serious view of putting the United States into a multi-polar group. At the same time, while China achieves affluence by cooperation with the USA amidst a globalised economy, it tries to soothe the US from perceiving excessive danger.

Politically and diplomatically such factors as a possible change in the situation in the Korean peninsula, occasioned by collapse of North Korea, China-Taiwan relations, and the worsening relationship with India and Japan may cast shadows onto the brightly lit Chinese grand strategy.

Just now the Chinese professor mentioned about the visit of President Obama to China, and had a joint communiqué. The reason why these two countries agreed was because China wants to be one of the countries who holds a share in world affairs, and also in regional and domestic issues. But, on the other hand it is important to know that President Obama did not mention about Chinese human rights, minority policies and also did not ask for transparency in military upgradations.

Can hegemony be reduced peacefully or not?

China aims at being an economic power and a military power, and eventually "a wealth and power" state. To attain this aim China intends to become a regional power in Asia first, with the objective of becoming a power in the world equal to the US. Now, China is at the same level as that of Japan's GDP, but in next fifteen years, Chinese GDP would be equal to that of the USA. In the process of becoming an economic power, there would be friction with the international community over the scramble for resources and the rules of the market.

On the way to becoming a military power, China attempts to instill fear into countries of the world with its space and missile strategy. It is also upgrading cyber-terrorism capability and strengthening, and modernising its conventional forces by focussing on the PLA Navy and Air Force. The Chinese Communist Party has been insisting that China is right in every respect, and that other parties are wrong with regard to any wars and disputes between China and the neighbouring countries post World War II. This unyielding stance will continue. The theory of justifying disputes and China being always in the right will be created by China and repeatedly insisted upon to the world community.

The time when economic growth becomes stagnant, public security becomes disorderly, and the people's dissatisfaction with the Communist Party becomes aggravated deserves attention. Presently, there is a lot of dissatisfaction amongst people in China against the Chinese Central Policy, and Chinese top leaders are having problems, not only in oversees political and economic policy but mainly due to domestic issues. It requires attention whether China would choose a way of becoming a cooperative partner in the future in the arena of international politics, or becoming an element of confusion.

At the end of my brief, I would like to conclude by saying that China is facing a dilemma. It has to decide whether China would be a good stake holder in international, regional and domestic issues or would it be going on her own way to pursue 'one' Communist Party rule. We ask of China to come together with us to share the responsibility of solving all the global, regional and domestic issues jointly.

Discussion - Session I

Issue Raised

The increase in protest rallies in China progressively year after year indicates dichotomy between their political system and market system of economy being pursued today. What steps are being taken to bring about political reforms to remove this dichotomy?

Responses

(a) China's concept is, 'socialist economy with Chinese characteristics'. This system combines 'market economy' and Chinese 'socialist politics'. China's development model is unique because it tries to accommodate market economy, which is very popular in globalised world today. So far it has helped the Chinese people to meet their development challenges successfully. They have the wisdom to adjust to such challenges and problems.

(b) The number of Chinese participating in the protests is very high – 1000 to 3000 people participate in each incident, which numbered 1,40,000 last year. This compelled the Chinese Central Party School to initiate a project which has suggested that they need to move away from some of the pitfalls of the 'market economy'. Firstly, they suggested the 'marketisation of politics' or 'politicisation of the market'. Between these two phenomena the Communist Party today is also suggesting that the 'protestors go to the court' – to the Peoples Proletariat, to deflect the protests and criticisms away from them. Secondly, at the village level, elections are conducted in 800,000 villages. However, the key problem is that the Communist Party base is at the 'county' level and not at the village level. Therefore, 'county' level is crucial but they are not conducting elections at the 'county' level. So that is one lacuna in the political reforms process. Since the 'one' person elected at the village elections will either become a 'leader' in the Communist Party or is already a 'member' – democratisation is limited in that respect.

(c) In China, democracy would not be like the Indian democracy. It will be a democracy with Chinese characteristics.

Issue Raised

What is the state of 'Confucianism' being adopted in China today? Since the value system suggested by sage Confucius has helped the Chinese in affecting many improvements and managing their economy so well, is it possible to adapt such a good system in India?

Responses

(a) In China there are no religious beliefs. The Communist Party members have no Gods. But ordinary people, who are apprehensive about their future because of social developments and uncertainties, can be seen going more and more to the temples – with some fear in their hearts, to pray for their well being and happiness. But it is quite different for other countries. Confucian values are important in Chinese people's daily lives. Chinese people go to temples to seek personal happiness in their daily lives and not because of Confucian values or being religious.

(b) The Chinese leadership follows the legalistic tradition and the people follow Confucian values whereby they seek harmony and happiness in their lives. Hu Jin Tao's 'harmonious world' is also derived from that. From the point of view of the 'grand strategy', the Chinese leadership follows Tao's philosophy and also takes the hard way of 'politics' by considering all things across the world and their Country.

(c) On the foreign policy front, Confucianism is at the top of the framework, with Taoism and Buddhism also in it. Inside this framework, there are many schools of thought. While, discussing Chinese foreign policy and grand strategy, we can talk of one Tao i.e. The Emperor's Way, but it is not realistic either to impose or expect China to accept any other system. In the international arena, 'harmony' is central terminology but 'Confucianism' is the essential framework in its foreign policy relationships with other countries.

Issue Raised

Is the current Communist Party ideology supportive and conducive to a 'stand alone' economic and military power?

Response

The influence of Party ideology is mainly on the communist party members. The economic growth, the military modernisation and social policy depend on Government policies and not on Party ideology. Ideology is a philosophy which provides political direction to the whole Country, and not for giving detailed economic or military policies.

Issue Raised

It seems that China loves 'one ruling party' system and is also talking about Chinese political democratisation. Now, when the world is looking forward to China becoming politically a democratic country, what are the conditions which would facilitate transition of China into a politically democratic country or would it continue to prefer 'one ruling party' system?

Responses

(a) Democracy is a very big concept. Different countries have different mechanisms to promote democracy. Democracy can be a way of life, it can be a political system and it can be a philosophy. In China, 'one ruling party' system has lasted for a long time. It has it's own reasons for having one ruling party because of historical background and political characteristics. Therefore, in near term, 'one ruling party' system is likely to continue.

(b) In China, there are some political reforms underway even within the one ruling party system. It is called 'inner democratisation'. There are some improvements in election procedures to have more candidates to select from or compete for the posts.

(c) Although China has one ruling party but there are other agencies to check the policies of the ruling party. The Chinese political system is so unique that it cannot copy any other democratic political party systems which are complicated, big and different. Chinese people do not want a multi-polar and multi-party political system; these are not considered feasible. We must respect the existing situation and Chinese characteristics while considering the process of political democratisation.

Issue Raised

The Quadrilateral Cooperation Proposal from Australia involving the USA, Australia and Japan, with the idea of bringing all the democracies together in a value based cooperation, was quite obviously directed against China. Since India had reservations on this proposal, what is the current Indian thinking on it?

Response

The proposal came in the context of new awareness on the growing Chinese influence and role. Unfortunately, the proposal was seen to have been designed to create a group of countries which excluded China in this part of the world. Any arrangement in this part of Asia which excludes China, and creates another group, was obviously going to run into difficulties. Rightly, the Chinese were the first to indicate their displeasure and anxiety; and questioned why it was being done? The Chinese showed that they were not happy, as the move was seen to be designed to isolate China. Therefore, the proposal went into a terminal situation. It indicates that China's growing influence and objections, did put a spoke into some of the proposals. Although before the Indian side could indicate, whether it was willing or not, the proposal got scuttled.

Issue Raised

What is the Chinese perspective on 'Rising India'? How are they viewing India's role in South Asia economically, strategically, and in its relationships with other countries in the region? Is it possible for both the countries to work together in future to evolve some cooperative strategies at various levels?

Responses

(a) Firstly, China is happy in the 'Rise of India' because it will bring some benefits to them also through economic cooperation. Secondly, both China and India can contribute to the establishment of the Asian community by reviving their ancient civilisations. Thirdly, China recognises that India can play a dominant role in the Asian region including South East Asia, East Asia and Central Asia. But China would appreciate more if India plays a constructive role in terms of economic development, political and regional stability. China sees an increase in this kind of role in the coming years and supports it. China has cooperated with India in some regional organisations, like Shanghai Cooperation Organisation (SCO), Asia Pacific Economic Cooperation (APEC) and other institutions.

(b) However, China has a history of having different views about development in the Asia Pacific Region and would like to discuss its role further in this regard.

(c) At the global level, China has very much similar positions and interests as other countries on issues such as climate change, environment protection etc.

(d)   China has clearly stated that it supports India's greater role in the international community, including the UN Security Council. This is what is stated by the top leaders in their meetings and joint statements. China does not want to be an obstacle in India's entry into the UN Security Council. But, because UN Council reforms are so complicated, presently there is no consensus on what kind of country can become a new Security Council member. If China gives clear support for India, it would raise complications in China's relations with Japan, Pakistan, Germany and other countries. It is also suggested that if a country wants to play a more important role in international community, before that, it would be better if it first plays a constructive role in the regional and global affairs. A new Security Council member does not mean that it has more 'rights' or 'power'. It means that the possibilities of enhanced duties towards the international community would increase in the future.

(e) India and China are very important rising powers in the Asian region. Close economic, political and military relations between them will bring peace and prosperity to the region. If there are problems that remain unresolved, then the region will not prosper.

Session I: Chairman's Closing Remarks

Ambassador MK Rasgotra

China's 'grand strategy', has been explained at length and I will say nothing about it. In my study of China's policies, nations do not always mean what they say. Stated policy is one thing, policies that are pursued in actual practice are at variance with stated objectives. China understandably, wants to be G1- Number One power in Asia – it is an understandable ambition. It wants to be G2 in the world with the United States of America. This is also an understandable ambition. Eventually, it may wish to become G1, but there are many question marks there. So far as India is concerned, my mind goes back to mid 1950's when Jawahar Lal Nehru was vigorously propagating the idea of *'India-China Bhai-Bhai'* at Bandung. The Chinese Premier Zhao en Lai met Mohammad Ali of Pakistan and told him, *"We have very serious problems with India. It's a difficult country. It's a big country. We are going to have problems with India. Since, you have problems with India, you and we should get together."* That is the beginning of their de facto alliance.

Chinese say that India is a rising power in South Asia. The objective is to confine and box India in South Asia. We need not quarrel with it. I mean they have this objective. We will concede this objective, but we will see what happens in the end. The time to watch in any period in history is when new powers are rising. It is a time of uncertainty, instability, contention; requiring new adjustments, so on and so forth.

During China's revolution and stabilisation, first thirty years after 1950, was the period of consolidation of revolutionary achievements. It was also a period of several wars - China's intervention in Korea, China's war on Vietnam, China's war with India in 1962, China's skirmishes with Russia. One hopes that history will not be repeated. But we have to understand China's economic rise and military strengthening. Peaceful economic rise and military modernisation go hand in hand – one reinforcing the other. What I am saying is stated very clearly by the Chinese 'policy makers'.

We had a study done on this subject in the Observers Research Foundation (ORF) and we came to a conclusion that Chinese want to increase their military strength because they want economic expansion. National policies of governments in power are geared to one basic objective, *'Promotion of the National interest'*. I think that applies to China of today as it applies to china of yore. I think in today's World, China will pursue its National interest, but conflict will arise when it seeks to pursue its National interest at the expense of or trespassing the National interest of other major countries in the region – Russia, India, Japan and South Korea to name a few.

In the case of India, the China-Pakistan alliance and the military cooperation between the two countries contributes to prolonging the avoidable and unnecessary confrontation between India and Pakistan. China's moves in the power game for example are efforts that are meant to undermine India's deep, close historic, geographic and cultural relations with that country. We will have to deal with that. At the same time we would not like to come in conflict with China.

We want a relationship of friendship with China – economic and commercial cooperation. China is a challenge in strategic terms, hopefully not in the military terms in the long run, provided we prepare ourselves for any kind of eventuality. But there is an opportunity. If China grows prosperous, I think that prosperity will spread around in the neighbourhood, in Asia.

My only concern is that in the present pursuit of multi-polarity or poly centricity, China will not ignore that, not just in the world, but within Asia also multi-polarity exists today. This is going to remain. If China's rise is entirely peaceful, everybody will want to be friends with China. But if China continues to assert itself militarily, through daily pin pricks, which is totally unnecessary and avoidable, it will bring no gain to it.

Our Prime Minister in his own very moderate and modest language said, "China's assertiveness – I don't know why China feels it is necessary?" There is this assertiveness in relation to India and towards Japan. If this continues, then there is bound to be tension. Tension may not lead to conflict hopefully, but tensions in Asia are not a happy development, especially between two large countries. We are not in competition with China. I think it was stated very clearly that China is number one in economic and military terms and it will remain so for many years to come. We wish China well, but any kind of avoidable, unnecessary, unprofitable assertiveness vis-à-vis India will only give rise to tension. I hope that will not be the story.

China today is an open country. It is no longer 'a land of mystery', as it was fifty years ago or hundred years ago or several centuries ago. China states its policies very clearly. Sometimes the underlying objectives are not very clear but a closer study of what they say in words does reveal their objectives. It is a good thing that our scholars like Professor Kondapalli (and others) and former diplomats are engaged in the study of China. Our commercial and business leaders are also becoming interested in China and I appreciate very much that USI has organised this Seminar. I hope that there will be many more such interactions in future.

I thank personally General PK Singh for associating me with this particular Session. I thank all the Panellists.

Thank you.

CHINA'S EMPLOYMENT OF SOFT POWER

SECOND SESSION

Chairman   Vice Adm KK Nayyar, PVSM,AVSM
                    (Retd) Former Vice Chief of Naval Staff

First Paper   Shri Mohan Guruswamy,
                    Centre for Policy Initiatives

Second Paper   Ms Bethany Danyluk,
                    Associate at Booz Allen Hamilton, USA

Third Paper   Professor Aileen Baviera,
                    University of the Philippines.

Fourth Paper   Shri Jayadeva Ranade, IPS (Retd)

Discussion

Session II : Chairman's Opening Remarks

Vice Admiral KK Nayyar, PVSM, AVSM (Retd)
Former Vice Chief of Naval Staff

Good afternoon ladies and gentlemen, I always take the post lunch attendees in these seminars as people who are seriously wedded to the subject. Many years ago, while speaking at RAND in Santa Monica I was questioned that some of my facts were not right. What I had said was that if a country 2200 years ago decided to build a wall 6000 km long, 20 ft wide, 20 ft high and then carried on building it for 1900 years, then we ought to be taking anything which they said and did very seriously. That perhaps explains the overkill of five or six seminars in a period of less than 10 days in Delhi on China. But having said that, we should take very seriously what the Chinese do and say. There is no other way to describe the bellicose statements which have emanated officially and semi-officially from Beijing. Therefore, I wonder whether we have not been generous in saying 'opportunities' in the title of this seminar, because there is 'strategic challenge', alright. I do hope that the climate changes and may be some opportunities would also arise. But the serious demeanour of Chinese has not given us hope of many opportunities in the offing. We are very lucky to have this distinguished panel to deal with the challenges, and opportunities if they see any, this afternoon.

Session II : First Paper

Shri Mohan Guruswamy

There is tremendous economic activity going around all over the world. As a matter of fact there are 63 countries today in the world which are growing at over 6 per cent. When we grow at 7 per cent, we get very excited. Please note that out of 63 other countries that are growing over 6 per cent, some unlikely countries like Ethiopia are growing at 11 per cent. The fastest growing country in the world is Bhutan which is growing at 24.6 per cent. Growth rate by itself, as our Prime Minister said, is not the entire game. Naturally, he would say that because our growth rates have not been too good compared to China. But even after making allowances for various factors, I would say that 6 per cent growth rate is no big deal anymore because developing world is growing at that pace. The important thing is that the world is changing rapidly.

Coming to the main part of my talk, how do we keep our foreign exchange reserves? Bulk of our reserves are kept in Dollars. Next is Euro which is about 27 per cent. Whatever we say and do, our money is kept in Western institutions. Many countries have tried to breach this monopoly of the Dollar, which arrived after World War II. Only the European Union (EU) has been able to make some inroads into it. That is because the EU as a whole has a GDP which is more than the USA. Even they could not do very much. Dollar is pretty much the king and whoever has to live in this world has to factor that into account. In terms of actual current percentages – 64 per cent of reserves were in US Dollar in 2008, 27 per cent in Euro, rest do not matter – German Mark, British Pound, Japanese Yen and Swiss

Franc, amounting to 3 per cent only. We would like to keep our money in Swiss banks but in Dollars and others upto 2 per cent. So, nobody is holding money in any other currency. That is why USA is the most important country in the world in economic terms. It is the engine of the world's economy – it is the driver of the world's economy. Because the US consumes so much, rest of our economies do well. We are pretty dependent on the US to keep this growth rate going. To think that the end of the US has come is a little premature. They are there to stay for quite some time to come.

How much money does a State have to spend? The size of per capita income of the USA is $ 46,000. Even, as China and India rise, if you take this projection upto the next 50 years i.e. to 2060, the US will still be number one spender with per capita income close to $ 100,000 – that will give them per capita tax revenue of about $ 25000. China's tax revenue per capita today is about $ 330, India's about $ 120 – the USA's is $ 8800. That is the real index of power not how many ships you have, how many guns you have. The USA will continue to be, at least in this Century, the *foremost economic power* in the world. They are in the forefront of technological advances in the world – computers, medicine, aerospace, advanced military equipment etc. Though this advantage has narrowed but they are still way ahead. That is why the world does well because they have a trade deficit of $ 847 billion with the USA.

Ironically, China's unprecedented economic rise and huge accumulation of wealth overseas, particularly in the USA in the form of US securities has created the first major challenge to what seemed an unimpeded rise to dominant status in the world. It is now caught in a deadly economic embrace with the USA – akin to Siamese twins. China has a trade surplus of almost $ 400 billion, out of which $ 303 billion worth is with the USA. What would happen to China if it did not have this trade surplus? There will be a hole in China's GDP which it cannot fill. India has a trade surplus with the USA. Every second country in the world has trade surplus with the USA. The number of countries who have a trade deficit with the USA is just a handful because they are quite ridiculously ill managed economies to have a trade deficit with the USA. This is how big the USA is – out of the total world GDP of about $ 56 trillion, the US is $ 14 trillion. Their GDP is growing at 2 per cent, but 2 per cent on $ 14 trillion is not the same as 10 per cent on $ 1 trillion, nor 11 per cent on $ 2.8 trillion. There is a big difference. The annual accrual here is huge. So, those who think that an end of the era has come, are again making a big mistake.

Why is the USA in trouble? When George Walker Bush took over, the US economy had a budget surplus of about $ 100 billion. That is what Bill Clinton left him because he was managing the economy well. He left them with a surplus. Look what happened after that? You had budgetary deficit, trade deficit – all just kept going up. Mr Obama had to pick up the reigns from here and he has barely been able to control the situation. Presently, the trade scenario in the USA is that they have current balance of $ 800 billion – *adverse*. They have exports of 1.15 per cent. If you look at their exports, aircraft and telecommunications amount to 49 per cent of their exports. Boeing alone is exporting about 30 per cent. While they export these to all the countries, they import from China 17 per cent. Why do they import from China? We will come to that. Almost all countries have got trade surpluses with the USA, except countries like the UAE, Hong Kong, Belgium, Australia. What are they buying from the Chinese? They are buying cheap electrical machinery, fans and other small things like apparel. As a matter of fact the USA imports $ 12 billion worth of Chinese shoes every year.

These days wherever you meet people from Asia they talk of transfer of power coming towards Asia. There is a new kind of power building up in the world. The power of monopsony i.e. when you have only one or two buyers. A monopoly is when you have only one manufacturer; but when you have only one or two buyers it is equally dangerous. The USA has arrived at a monopsonous position on many articles with China, and it is a monopoly supplier of many 'leading technology' articles. If you want to buy a Boeing plane, it is $ 400 million per piece. If you want to buy Intel chips, they will decide the price. So they are monopoly suppliers and monopsnous buyers. Therefore, they are very comfortably placed economically.

Amongst the world's top exporters, Germany is No.1, then, it is China, the USA and Japan. These are the big export players in the world. China's trade with the USA is growing. The USA exports amount to $ 72 billion and imports to $ 338 billion. Every year percentage change kept going up till 2008, and then it dropped. That is the cause of China's troubles. If USA's exports and imports figures get more and more balanced, China would get squeezed. So, China's soft power, hard power, smart power is not going to work because everything is working because of a hole in Uncle Sam's trade balance. If that gets closer, you are in deep trouble. Chinese lost 22 million jobs since the slowdown of the world economy. Exports are dropping at the rate of 10-12 per cent per quarter. This quarter it dropped 13.1 per cent. So, I cannot see how you are going to recover without the USA becoming profligate again. There is a moral there – if the US health gets better, China's health gets bad.

China's trade with the world has led to the remarkable rise of China. In 10 years it has gone up almost eight to ten folds. The USA gives you a large market so you get economies of scale. When you get those economies of scale you can pretty much do what you want with other markets. Now in India we have a bilateral trade of 55 billion $ with China and Chinese have a trade balance of $ 12 billion in their favour. If you go to the market in India today, everything comes from China. The Chinese are exporting with those economies of scale all over the world. Amongst China's top trading partners, we are somewhere at No 11. But the USA is right at the top.

The world economy is growing fast. It was 3.6 per cent, touched almost 4 per cent in 2008, before coming to a halt. Again it is picking up and it will keep rising. This era is one of fast economic growth for the developing world. In this Asia is growing fastest. Asia's share of world GDP exceeds EU, the USA and rest of the world. If Asia unites together to get a common currency, then may be, it can challenge the Dollar but not till then. But Asia consists of Japan which is not very fond of China, it consists of India also not very fond of China, ASEAN which is very suspicious of China, and then we do not like each other very much. Asia leads the world in growth. They are stashing away money abroad, in Swiss Banks. Are they going to start putting money in Yuan or Yen, very unlikely.

The excitement in the world is all about future growth. The Goldman Sachs have predicted future growths for India, the USA and China. The rest are pretty much there, but, they do not really factor – Japan, Britain, Russia, UK, Germany and France. Actually India is sitting on the verge of a far greater growth opportunity than China is. As a matter of fact next year and the year afterwards, India's growth rates will be more than China's, because there is a demographic push coming in for India's growth rate. Whether we handle our economy well is another thing. But the window of opportunity starts to open up very soon.

In the recent days there is much talk of BRICs – Brazil, Russia, India, China. BRICs is being favoured as a new power. The Chinese are very keen on exploring BRICs as an alternate source, as a stabilising instrument, as a different source of power to challenge the US hegemony and the Dollar. In BRICs India has the highest potential. As this period goes we will be growing two per cent more than China. As a matter of fact, if you do one per cent more then you actually overtake China in GDP terms in 2040 or so. That possibility is now beginning to dawn on the world. If you add 2 per cent you are well past China by 2030. And we are already on the +2 per cent trajectory. +2 per cent trajectory we said is very difficult, very optimistic but we are already doing it. Goldman Sachs said, China is going to do 5.8 per cent, we are doing 7.8 per cent, when they say they are going to do 9 per cent, we will be doing 11 per cent. Prime Minister is already talking about 11 and I see that is possible. But, whether we are going to have equitable growth, a balanced growth !! I do not know.

In the rapidly changing world, a new world order is emerging. In this situation, how does the world get off the Tiger? The obvious answers are: If the USA lives within its means, China slows down. If China slows down, the US lives within its means. This is a symbiotic relationship. As a matter of fact the US economists describe their relationship as one between that of a drug addict and a drug peddler, or a dope addict and a dope peddler. One needs to sell the dope, the other keeps consuming it – I describe them as Siamese twins, joined together with different personalities. Both are fighting and shouting at each other but have to eat at the same time because they have one stomach. If the USA has to live within its means: -

(a) It has to pull out of these wars.

(b) Balance its budget and trade with China.

(c) Force the revaluation of the Yuan. Otherwise this means, curbing dollarisation of the world, increasing special drawing rights (SDR's).

(d) BRICs bilateral trading, in own currencies. This is a possibility. Suppose I trade with China, China buys and pays me in Yuan and I pay them back in Rupee. We have the same currency, we hold our own currency as reserves against each other. China is already doing it with Brazil. But suppose we start doing it on a larger scale, it might challenge dollarisation.

(e) Then you might have ASEAN, economic blocks i.e. China-India-Japan as one economic block. Why not? European Union is already there.

(f) G 20 is the IMF. It should take control of the IMF to ensure closer monitoring of members with the mandate of having balanced trade in accordance with Brettonwood Compact prescriptions.

Why did this imbalance take place? Because, both China and the USA breached the Brettonwoods Compact which talked about having balanced trade. Both of them have got good economists who studied in each other's universities, yet they breached their Brettonwoods Compact. If you want to get back to normalcy you have to balance your budgets, and your trade. The slogan I give is, *'balance or perish'*. But who will bell the big cat? I do not think Dr Manmohan Singh is going to do it, I do not think Hu Jintao is going to do it, I do not think Obama is going to do it. Today, the world is a patient with a big deep wound and Mr Obama is applying band aid to it. It can check bleeding for a little while. But if you do not balance your trade, you don't balance your books, do not slow the Chinese down, the bleeding is going to start again and we would be in bad trouble. The next time it bleeds it will bleed down.

Session II : Second Paper

Ms Bethany Danyluk

China's employment of soft power is an extremely broad topic and open to analysis through a number of different approaches. I tried to break it down into its component parts and analyse these parts in a way that complements that of my fellow panel members. In doing so, I am going to focus mainly on China's use of soft power in the developing world and particularly in Africa and Latin America. I will start by introducing what soft power is and by clarifying my interpretation of soft power for the purposes of this conference. I will then talk about why China is using soft power primarily in the developing world and what is it hoping to achieve. After that I will briefly assess the extent to which China's soft power has been successful in achieving its national objectives and move on to a discussion on the implications of China's employment of soft power for the rest of the world and also for China itself. Finally, I will conclude some perspectives on what China's future soft power strategy might look like.

First, what is soft power? As you probably are aware the term soft power was coined by the scholar Joseph Nigh in his book 'The Changing Nature of American Power' which was published in 1990. But subsequent interpretations have expanded this definition somewhat and I will get to that in a moment but first I would like to read a short excerpt from Nigh in which he defines soft power by distinguishing it from hard power. He says, "a state may achieve the outcomes it prefers in world power stakes because other states want to follow it or have agreed to a situation that produces such effect. In this sense it is just as important to set the agenda and structure the situations in world politics as to get others to change in particular cases. The second aspect of power which occurs when one country gets other countries to want what it wants, might be called cooptive or soft power in contrast with the harder command power of ordering others to do it at once." Nigh then goes on to point out the three sources of soft power – culture, ideology and institutions. As scholars have continued to develop this theory an expanded definition of soft power has taken shape to include additional components such as economics and diplomatic engagement. Josh Kurlantzick, a renowned scholar at the Carnegie Endowment in Washington, authored the book 'China's Charm Offensive' and wrote in 2006 that today in the Asian context, soft power is understood to imply all elements outside the security realm including investment aid. So, I submit to you that this definition applies in the context of other regions as well, including Africa, the Middle East, South and Central Asia and Latin America. The dominating theme of the panel questions derive from the economic question surrounding China's use of soft power. So, I think it is safe to say that we can invoke this expanded definition for the purposes of this conference panel. But I don't want to do that to the exclusion of the other factors. So, I want to use the definition of soft power that is broad enough to include the important economic dimension but restrictive enough to adhere to Nigh's original principles.

This brings me to the four specific tools that I will be talking about as China uses them for soft power purposes. *First*, economic engagement refers to interactions with other states in terms of trade, investment and aid, and other incentives and these last three usually intertwine and are often hardly distinguished from each other.

Second is public diplomacy characterised by how China basically advertises itself or what I will refer to as its public relations (PR) campaign that also includes visits and exchanges by leaders and delegations from other countries and symbolic agreements that are usually intended to demonstrate how successful these visits and exchanges are. *Third*, participation in multilateral institutions. This describes China's use of regional or global organisations to shape behaviour and outcomes in ways that promote its interests. And *fourth*, dissemination of culture includes sponsorship of cultural, sport events, education initiatives to promote Chinese language and culture, and the Chinese diaspora itself. It also includes use of Chinese media to promote its image and increase tourism.

So, why is China using soft power? China is pursuing a national strategy to increase its comprehensive national power which includes both hard and soft components. So, while China is modernising its military as we are all aware it is also focussing on the other side of the equation. Along the way China has several intermediate goals aimed at promoting a peaceful environment that will not interfere with China's development. *First* and foremost, it wants to protect territorial sovereignty which describes its pursuit of the One China Policy. *Second*, China needs to look outward for energy and raw materials to sustain its high levels of growth and this goal is particularly important because economic growth is the key of the legitimacy of the regime and failure to sustain this growth would portend instability in China. *Third*, China advocates multi-polarity which implies a world in which the USA is no longer the global hegemon. *Fourth*, China hopes to gain political support from other countries to back its positions in international institutions. Then another reason for China's increasing use of soft power is that China's employment of hard power strategies have not been particularly effective over the past few decades. Juxtaposed with the success of the US policies at the height of American appeal internationally China realised that it was necessary to look for new ways to achieve its goal. Seeing this, China simply turned and changed policy offering assistance and wanting friends wooing, not intimidating, would now be the order of business. Finally, growing concerns among other actors with respect to China's military modernisation have encouraged Chinese leadership to emphasise more benign manifestations of its foreign policies.

So, casting its rise as non-threatening is particularly important to China and it is taking care to emphasise several themes designed to reinforce this point. This is actually part of its PR strategy that will be described later but I decided to introduce it here because it provides a helpful framework for thinking about the other elements of soft power. So, first China is pursuing a strategy of peaceful development that is benign in nature and not aimed at any particular country. Relationships with China are win-win characterised by mutual benefits. China aims to promote a harmonious world in which relationships are based on friendship, equality and mutual respect. China maintains a policy of non-interference in State's domestic affairs.

Let us look at China's soft power tools in a bit more detail. I am just going to touch on these. Economic engagement, trade, investment aid, increasing trading relations have made China and developing countries increasingly inter-dependent on each other. China's investments are aimed at developing energy and natural resources and infrastructure which is actually designed to facilitate its own acquisition of supplies to fuel its economy. China uses multilateral institutions to strengthen its international image, build legitimacy and credibility and show that it is interested in being a responsible stakeholder. China's status as a permanent member of the UN Security Council places it in a position to veto resolutions that undermine its interests as well as shape efforts at future reform.

It is also a member of the regional institutions which allows it a role in shaping the objectives of these organisations. China is also a founding member of groupings such as the SCO and the BRIC nations, and the China-Africa Forum which aim to balance the US influence and/or provide alternatives to engagement with the United States that are more focused on the interests of rising actors. China also uses public diplomacy, spends a lot of time on public relations to advertise its development as peaceful and good for the world and it maintains a full diplomatic agenda conducting visits, and exchanges between not only high level officials and delegations but lower level engagements with politicians, political parties and interest groups. These visits and exchanges are often accompanied by symbolic agreements and China has also been placing increasing emphasis on developing its diplomatic corps.

Cultural Diplomacy. While public diplomacy is designed to court elites, cultural diplomacy aims to advertise China to foreign public and to provide tangible evidence of China's goodwill. So, as I mentioned China sponsored cultural and sporting events, has tried to make it easier for foreign students to study in China, it has also developed computer institutes which are institutes that facilitate the global reach of Chinese culture and language. It has got very populous diaspora across the world, especially in developing countries, and also uses media and tourism.

So, how successful has China been in using soft power? There is no question that China has been somewhat successful in building and leveraging soft power in developing nations in pursuit of its overarching objectives. China has been able to increase its access to energy and raw materials overseas and to diversify the sources of these supplies. Only 23 countries remain which have official relations with Taiwan and experts have noted that developing countries are increasingly considering China's reactions when making decisions about their domestic affairs. Several factors however suggest that China's success might not be sustainable over the long term. Assessments from several years ago often cited results of respected opinion polls such as the PU Global Attitudes Report and the Chicago Council as indicators of China's success in soft power strategy. More recent findings of these polls however reflect a decrease in China's popularity and increasing negative perceptions among other countries. It is also unclear how valuable Chinese soft power has been in the UN. In the past, it has vetoed resolutions intended to isolate countries in which China has interests but more recently it has begun to support resolutions by condemning human rights abuses in places like Burma and Sudan. Finally, in Africa and Latin America where China is popular among the elites, resentment is building among the public in response to what they view China as a neo-colonial and exploitative practices. Latin American businesses are increasingly having to compete for market share of Chinese manufactured goods which are often sold below the market value. Investment projects are not translating into as many employment opportunities for local populations because China is importing its own workers and when it does employ local populations they often face sub-par conditions and low wages. China also tends to export its environmental practices creating further source of backlash.

This is a practical example of my experience with how China's soft power has been successful. It is actually an excerpt from a recent request for proposal issued by the US Agency for International Development to solicit contractor support for food and enterprise development programme in Liberia. It describes the guiding principles for the programme. I will read you the 7th guideline. "Pursue opportunities to collaborate with China: USAID, Liberia and Embassy of China are actively working to address opportune partnerships." Because of China's growing influence in Africa it is fuelling economic growth, helping the developing economies to stay afloat during the time of global recession, its investment support is badly needed in infrastructure and it is helping to establish it as a responsible stakeholder in international affairs which other countries are hoping to leverage to achieve the outcomes of mutual interest such as stabilising the global economy and reining in North Korea. Furthermore, China's participation in multilateral institutions means further integration with the international community which will hopefully lead to greater accountability and expectations of compliance with international norms. Alternatively, some consequences of China's soft power activities support outcomes that create a pretext for instability by undermining international norms and institutions empowering rogue or corrupt regimes and building a foundation that could support increased uses of hard power in future.

These are just a few of the implications that the rest of the world must consider and it is difficult to determine whether the good outweighs the bad because we don't know China's intentions are. But as Jasjit Singh pointed out in the beginning of the conference, may be it is not necessary that has to be an either/or situation and we can be prepared to embrace the good and work together to achieve common interests for devising strategies to deal with the challenges. We should also consider the implications of China's use of soft power for China itself. Beyond the previously discussed benefits of the strategy in meeting China's national objectives, it also makes China more vulnerable in several areas. *First*, resources being spent for developing soft power assets have receded means, there are fewer resources to devote to China's own internal development. Chinese economy as we know is growing rapidly but it lacks the infrastructure to support the pace and capacity of this growth. Despite China's statements that it does not have aspirations for a leadership role in the international community it could be compelled to assume one beyond the need to protect its own foreign interests. States already look to China to leverage its influence on issues of mutual interest and likely to pressure China to assume responsibilities in either ones, not for ones it is prepared.

As the Chinese presence and profile grow, China is likely to draw more scrutiny from the international community placing increased emphasis on its record of human rights, environmental practices and domestic weaknesses. Increased awareness of the Chinese dark side could tarnish its image and would neutralise or reverse the soft power successes that it has had, much like what happened to the US following the exposure of Abu Gharaib and enhanced interrogation techniques. I think this is already taking place in the case of bringing to light the situation of weaker population. I would imagine that up until a few years ago, the average American following of current events had no idea of what a veto was and now it has been in the news. So, the point to be made here is that the benefits China derives from successful employment of soft power are accompanied by costs that should not be ignored, either by China or the international community because countries have an interest in promoting stability in China; the prospects of instability are serious and far reaching.

Then, I will conclude with a look at perhaps what the future of the China soft power looks like which is quite intimidating with my Chinese colleagues in the audience because I don't presume to know more than they do, but just based on recent literature here is what I have to say. Experts hold competing views of whether China has an actual soft power strategy. Some argue that its use of soft power has been largely ad hoc and opportunistic and does not reflect a well thought out and planned approach. Others however contend that China has a strategy for everything so there is no possibility that this could not be part of their strategy. But regardless of its current state there have been indications that China is ready to pursue a strategic approach to its use of soft power, if it isn't already. Several themes emerge from the July 2009 Ambassadorial Conference that was attended by China's foreign policy leaders. First, President Hu specifically emphasised the importance of the role of soft power in Chinese foreign policy. He then laid out four goals that China should strive to further its foreign policy which subsequently became to be known as four strengths. They include: China should be a more influential power in politics, more competitive in the economic field, should have more affinity in its image and be a more appealing force in morality. I think you can see that the soft power characteristics of the four strengths are evident. The dynamics of the conference implied the intention to pursue more active foreign policy. So, China is moving away from a 'pull' approach by which a country is able to convince other countries to want what it wants to the 'push' approach where a country actually uses its political influence to compel other countries to do what it wants.

Over the past few decades China has followed Deng Xiaoping's approach to foreign policy characterised by the phrase, "*keep a low profile and bide your time while also getting something accomplished*". The documents from the July conference reveal a slightly nuanced version of the principle described as, "*Uphold keeping a low profile and biding our time more actively, getting something accomplished*". Chinese leadership subsequently affirmed this shift when Premier Wen Jiabao advocated for a new focus on what he called functional diplomacy. This approach is characterised by more involvement in cooperative structures that address the challenges such as climate change, maritime piracy and drug trafficking. As I thought about this idea it has become clear that this approach will inevitably blur the lines even further between soft and hard power. The functional diplomacy seems to me as basically a description of collective security or security cooperation and the challenges to be addressed clearly require the use of military capabilities. Think about China's recent anti-piracy operations off the coast of Somalia. This raises the question for further consideration and debate. How does the increasing intersection or ambiguity between hard and soft power, and China's foreign policy change the way we think about the future security environment and whether China is an opportunity or a challenge?

Session II : Third Paper

Professor Aileen Baviera

My brief this afternoon is to talk to you about China's soft power in South East Asia. First of all, I need to begin with a caveat that South East Asia is a very diverse region, diverse in many ways including in its responses and actions towards China. Just as China's attitudes and policies in South East Asian countries also may have some differences between them, so it is difficult to generalise South East Asia in that sense. Nonetheless through years of our community building and relating to each other and gradually harmonising our foreign policy attitudes, if not foreign policy itself, you might say that the South East Asian countries do have some shared concerns about the rise of China and as a consequence also about the role of China as a new regional and global power.

In terms of soft power China's influence in South East Asia has often been said to have grown rapidly in recent years and in fact in the last few years there have been a number of scholars from the US and Japan also coming to South East Asian countries, exploring this subject matter: Has China's influence really grown that much; to what extent has this taken place and is it going to be at the expense of the US and Japanese influence specifically? So, it is considered an important subject. My presentation is going to be a preliminary exploration of the following questions. In what specific areas of soft power has China's influence been observed to grow in South East Asia? What factors might occur for such trends and will this influence be at the expense of other powers?

Bethany has already given a definition of soft power. Let me just reiterate very briefly that in my study I looked at the elements of soft power as inclusive of culture, economics, human capital, diplomacy and politics. My conclusion which I would like to state at the outset is that China's soft power diplomacy has been most effective in the economic and the diplomacy arena but not as effective and may have very little impact as far as culture, human capital and politics is concerned in the South East Asian region.

Why has China's diplomacy been so successful in South East Asia? There are a number of milestones to this. Perhaps, the most pronounced and some of you may remember that up to the mid-90s there was a lot of suspicion among the South East Asian states about China, particularly actions that China had taken in the South China Sea as well as across the Taiwan straits. It is very significant that in the 1997-98 Asian financial crisis China was ready and generous with its assistance to the specific South East Asian countries that were most affected while other powers or other international financial institutions were not quite ready to come to the assistance of these countries. So, the perception of China as a responsible stakeholder, as a partner for regional development and stability really grew as a consequence of the Asian financial crisis. China did not only provide aid assistance but played an active role in the Chiang Mai currency swap initiatives and also supplying some credit for helping the regional economies by not devaluing the *renminbi*.

As of now, all South East Asian countries enjoy a trade surplus with China which is considered an advantage to them. In the concerns running up to China's membership in the WTO, when most South East Asian countries were afraid that this would result in a lot of diversion of trade to China rather than South East Asia, China took the initiative to offer the China-ASEAN Free Trade Area which was intended to reassure the South East Asian economies that they could participate just as well in the prosperity of China. There were many add-ons to this programme such as the early harvest programme giving advantages to the least developed economies of South East Asia. In other words, as far as its economic initiatives towards ASEAN or South East Asian countries were concerned, China was able to project itself as a responsible stakeholder and an economic leader.

On other initiatives, China was the first to sign on to the Treaty of Amity and Cooperation in South East Asia when other great powers were still reticent about this, it entered into strategic partnership not only with the ASEAN as a whole but with each individual country. Some of the strategic partnership agreements had defence cooperation elements to them indicating how much had changed by way of the perceptions of China's security role in the region. There was a lot of bilateral assistance particularly to Cambodia, Laos and Myanmar and the message of this high level political agreements also was that China was prepared to commit long term to the peace and stability of the region and that it conceived itself as shaping the destiny of South East Asia. There was also a Declaration of Conduct in the South China Sea that was signed by China and ASEAN which on China's side was intended to demonstrate that it could have a reasonable and flexible approach from its earlier insistence on dealing with these territorial issues bilaterally towards a multilateral dialogue on this issue, though it is also observed that in more recent times China has been backtracking in fact from the multilateral discussions on territory and reverting back to bilateral discussions. There were energy cooperation agreements with a number of countries. I think most of all China has consistently stated its strong support for the central role that ASEAN plays in regional community building initiatives and has participated actively in multilateral regimes and institutions in the East Asian region which includes ASEAN+3, the ASEAN Regional Forum, the East Asia Summit, all ASEAN RIM and ASEAN centred arrangements as well as of course APEC. Through its participation in this ASEAN RIM and regional arrangements China's message has been that it is against hegemony, it is inclusive based and it distinguishes itself from the unilateralist approach of other powers, primarily the USA and Japan.

So, while this successful diplomacy and the charm offensive were taking place, there were other factors that aided primarily the low credibility of the US in South East Asia. At the time, following successive government's apparent disinterest in the region, the post-9/11 unilateralist policies of the Bush government and the military approach to terrorism were not received well in South East Asia – where we have predominantly Muslim states in Indonesia, Malaysia, Brunei and significant minorities in Thailand and Philippines. The military approach to terrorism post 9/11 antagonised many republics in the region. So, you can see the declining popularity of the USA and the increasing popularity and influence of China. Japan's continued economic woes may have been a factor although it must also be said that Japan by far still remains the major economic partner as far as the great powers go and its influence is not always politically communicated. But it is very much part of the regional and national economies and it will be there to stay. Then there is also a media treatment of China's economic success stories all over which helps create a positive attitude towards China in the region. In the economic and diplomatic initiatives this has been quite successful.

Is China's cultural soft power growing? Perhaps, among the ethnic Chinese in South East Asia this may be said to be true. There is interest in learning the Chinese language and the culture especially among second/third generation ethnic Chinese, who have very little roots to China as the motherland – but not much beyond ethnic Chinese communities. You will understand that there have always been important Chinese communities in these countries. Chinese culture is neither new nor exotic or exciting. We are very familiar with Chinese culture. China's rise does have a cultural element but I believe it has minimal impact on the countries of the region. In comparison when you look at young people they are probably more attracted to the Japanese and Korean pop culture. There is much admiration for high Chinese culture, cinema for instance, as well as China's achievements in science and technology of late. A lot of bad media coverage on its tainted products is also affecting opinion of China, like in the Philippines for instance, where many of the Chinese imports available in supermarkets are considered of inferior quality. If not due to anything else but the traders themselves are going for the cheaper goods not necessarily the best quality ones. While you have the prospect of a rising China militarily and economically, on the other hand, the level of exposure among the ordinary people also projects a negative sign to China's economic rise.

Is the attraction of Chinese politics growing in South East Asia? There was a time in the late 1980s and 90s when we had this debate about Asian values and how human rights would be differently interpreted in East Asia and the so called Confucian societies as compared to the West. During that time you might say there was some attraction to a Confucian kind of politics and how development should not take place in democracy as far as the aspirations of the people of the region are concerned, but since then we have seen an increasing liberalisation of politics in South East Asia – the democratisation of Indonesia following fall of Suharto, in Thailand, in the Philippines. Even growing civil society role in Malaysia for instance would tend to an outcome where the kind of politics that China represents, authoritarian centralised politics, top-down decisions would not be considered attractive any more. So, among intellectuals for instance, if you talk about China it just does not have the same kind of attraction as it may have had in the late 1950s because of the internal developments in the region itself. Possible exception would be I suppose Singapore. Because of antipathy to one party system in the region you will see multiparty systems and political reforms taking place. Another negative projection of China is its involvement in corruption scandals in some of these countries. In Philippines for instance what would have been major big ticket investment projects became mired in allegations of corruption and had to be withdrawn or suspended. So, this also does not give good publicity or promotion to China.

In terms of China's human capital, Singapore obviously has a policy of attracting highly skilled Chinese professionals, academics, engineers. But in the case of the Philippines, we see continued Chinese migration of low skilled workers. So, despite the rise of China and its improving economy there are still significant numbers of Chinese who migrate and take low level jobs or end up as street sellers. That also gives a different image when we talk about Chinese power. Some of the new migrants are not even supported by the earlier migrants from China because they end up in business competition with each other. So, there are issues among the old and new migrants. Some of the new migrants become involved in illegal activities such as drug trafficking and this gets a lot of media attention again – projecting a negative image of the country.

Can China's soft power influence the behaviour of other states – independent of these States' perceptions of hard power? I think the exercise of soft power on the part of China has not at all led to the abandonment of hard power as an instrument. In South East Asia there continues to be concerns about China's military modernisation and its readiness to use force on the Taiwan issue. All the governments have committed to a one China policy. But because of the principle of using force in itself, when ASEAN in their collective ethics have spoken out very much in favour of peaceful settlement of disputes and non-military approach to conflicts in the region. Economic domination remains the concern of our specific industry sectors within South East Asia. Even Myanmar, which is perceived to be closest to China in political and economic interests, fears growing dependency. It is well known that New Delhi is also engaged in some balancing of sorts.

So, while the China's soft power does have an impact in terms of its diplomacy and economic influence, in other areas it is not as successful and still has some way to go to compete, even with the Japanese soft power in the South East Asian region – much less with western soft power, if you like. The South East Asian countries are very much engaged with

China in a comprehensive way much more than at any time in the past but in this period where we have seen this growing engagement between China and South East Asia we have also seen increased hedging by the same countries. Opportunities for hedging, especially which came about after 9/11, where the focus on terrorism gave new life to cooperation with the USA. Of course, many observers feel that this is not entirely about terrorism but there are some concerns about rising powers that come into the picture. It is observed that increase in soft power is occurring at the expense of influence of other powers, such as the USA. But there is hedging taking place, which means that there is a lot of increased confidence now, because China's policies are of a non-threatening nature and that there are more opportunities that can be built in developing good relations with China. At the same time the future role of China as a regional and global power still raises a lot of questions that remain unanswered. Therefore, the tendency to hedge against China's rise persists.

China's proactive stance has put pressure on the USA and Japan in their own dealings with South East Asia. For instance, it was only after the China-ASEAN Free Trade Area that Japan began to consider entering into the same kind of arrangements with South East Asia and the same with the USA. So, the indications are that they were reacting to China's growing inroads in the region. It remains the policy of ASEAN to engage all great powers to balance each other and to prevent the rise of any regional hegemon among them. The more China is engaged and the more China becomes a dominant player in South East Asia, both economically and in the security arena, the players of the ASEAN will work with other big players to remain engaged as well. We see this also in the regional community building efforts by the ASEAN+3 which includes South East Asia, China, Japan and Korea has been a very successful initiative for well over 10 years with solid contributions to regional economic stability. Still it was considered desirable by some major South East Asian countries to expand this into the East Asia Summit bringing in India, Australia and New Zealand – possibly the US also but again that remains up in the air.

I will end with a small note. By and large in South East Asia it is still largely hard power that rides the perceptions of China and not soft power. Without diluting the suspicions about Chinese hard power including fear of using its economic leverage down the line, it is doubtful whether China's charm offensive alone would turn around perceptions on China from its immediate neighbours in South East Asia.

Session II : Fourth Paper

Mr Jayadeva Ranade

I am the last speaker to follow three very competent and distinguished panelists who have discussed this subject at length. But I intend to use a broad brush analytical approach to discuss the application of soft power and cite a few examples on how China has actually used it. The phrase 'soft power' appears to be contradictory, but actually, this concept of non-military inducement has been around for many centuries and been enunciated by practitioners of state craft over the years in different regions and seen diverse applications. In this part of the globe, for example, we have had Chanakya and Sun Tzu both independently enunciating its fundamental principles. The original concept was to find a way to overawe, influence or seduce the adversary into accepting the superiority of the initiating power without recourse to force. That principle remains valid till today. To an extent it can be considered a derivative of psychological warfare. As a modern concept, however, soft power was formalised in its present form by Harvard University Professor Joseph Nigh. He explained soft power to mean, "A nation's ability to obtain international interests by exhibiting its inner attractions". He elaborated , "Not only great powers but other countries can also develop soft power which could exert more influence than military force on global matters".

In modern management parlance soft power would be akin to brand image. The two in fact are almost inter-changeable and the attributes of soft power are also intangible. They include a country's culture, language, music, cuisine, etc. At the same time in my opinion, soft power cannot be implemented unless it is backed by military, scientific and technological power strongly. Here, I will quote three examples which ideally depict the application of soft power in present times. Two of the countries that I have selected are not major economic or military powers; neither do they wield great political influence in world affairs and yet they have carved out a niche for themselves in international affairs solely on the basis of the method of application of soft power. The first country is Switzerland, a small country with an area of slightly over 40000 sq km and a population of under seven million. Switzerland appeared to be destined to remain on the outer fringes of international affairs. Yet, by following studied neutrality (a principle - it had no option but to adopt because of its size) symbolising the basis for a stable and sound economy, even in very disturbed times, Switzerland had projected itself as a safe and secure destination for storage of funds and bullion by individuals, large corporations and countries. This image directly benefits Switzerland because no country engaged in hostilities would want to jeopardise, the safety of its own financial security or that of its governing elite by attacking Switzerland. This is not a classic example of application of soft power but it has inherent in it the idea contained in the original concept. In any case by acquiring this brand image, Switzerland has acquired for itself a stature higher than what it could normally hope to aspire for.

The second example pertains to the use of soft power by a country in order to find a place for itself in international affairs that is Norway. Again a small country approximately 500,000 sq km mainly mountainous, population of under five million. It is geographically located on the periphery of world politics but has successfully converted its location into an asset. It is portrayed that its distance from the vortex of international politics actually gives it the objectivity necessary to mediate in conflicts and bring about a resolution. Norway has over the years sought to build an image of objectivity as a neutral mediator of conflicts and in the process again acquired an international stature bigger than it could normally hope for.

The USA is the final example and the concept of soft power as formulated by Joseph Nigh fits. As the USA gained in economic, military, scientific and technological strength, it expanded its global reach to project its power. This was a combination of military, diplomatic and soft power. The first attraction to people around the world was the economic opportunities afforded by the American economic strength and over the past couple of centuries this lured thousands of people from all over the world to the USA. A substantive acknowledgement of the US soft power is that in Chinese the US is called 'meco' or a beautiful country. Many of us would recall that numerous Chinese workers were employed in construction of the rail roads and many more followed in their wake setting up small laundry and shoemaking businesses – and finally China Towns all across the USA. This exodus of people into the USA and the money they sent home would have contributed to naming the US as 'meco'. Other more vivid examples of the American soft power familiar to people the world over are the Hollywood movies, American music and most of all the ubiquitous Coca Cola. Military, scientific and technological strength have played a major role as a number of countries sought to align themselves with the US for the benefits that could flow from proximity and USA's wealth and global influence.

But China too has in recent years grasped the usefulness of soft power and decided to employ it in the pursuit of its goals. The concept fits well with Confucian philosophy also and of other Chinese philosophers. I would not go into that aspect right now. But China's first concrete application of soft power was during the Asian Financial Crisis in 1997-98 when it did not devalue the Yuan despite pressure and took steps to assist the affected countries in the region. It's action appealed to the business and government elites in these countries and created a foothold for it. China's aid to countries in Africa is another concrete example of China converting its economic strength to soft power to achieve its strategic and diplomatic goals. Chinese aid annually totals 1.5 to 2 billion dollars to Africa. This has been backed by teams of doctors sent from China, scholarships to African students to study in China and projects that directly improve peoples' lives like railways, dams and power stations alongwith training programmes for military personnel of African countries. Chinese Premier Wen Jiabao at Sharm- El-Sheikh earlier in November this year offered Africa an additional 10 billion dollars in concessional loans over the next 3 years; thus, fulfilling Chinese President Hu Jintao's offer in 2006 to double the quantum of assistance. Africa as is well known is viewed by China as an abundant source of natural resources and soft power is being used here to achieve strategic goals.

The other area of strategic and direct interest for China is South East Asia. This is a region replete with potential flashpoints over territorial disputes and the presence of ethnic Chinese local overseas population. In the early 1990s, China assessed that it would find it difficult to recover its claimed offshore territories in the face of resistance from countries like Vietnam, the Philippines, Japan etc. It perceived that all the countries with contesting claims viewed China with suspicion and were trying to unite and oppose China. Accordingly, Beijing decided to adopt a policy to co-opt or soften each country individually. It decided to use diplomacy reinforced by economic strength. Culture, diplomacy, foreign aid, trade and investment were employed to soften popular and governmental suspicion of China as well as over shadow the US influence. China began disbursing large sums of aid and assistance to the South East Asian countries. It focussed on enhancing bilateral trade with the South East Asian nations to create a dependence on China's huge economy and domestic market. By 2006 China's over all trade with the region touched 160 billion US dollars. By the following year it had exceeded that of the USA. It is estimated to touch 1.2 trillion by 2010. China today has considerable influence in the region, thanks also to its economically powerful and wealthy overseas Chinese community in these countries.

It has pursued a similar policy in South Asia where it has used a combination of circumstances to build influence. Primarily, it has been willing to extend fiscal assistance, take up developmental projects and develop trade links. By 2010 China's bilateral trade with South Asia is estimated to exceed well over a 100 billion dollars. In addition, as in the case of most of the other countries where it has strategic interests, it has got involved in numerous infrastructure developmental projects that favourably project its image and earn good will.

What has been the effect of this soft power effort? A 2007, Pu Research Poll confirms that China's effort at using its strong economy as soft power to project a less threatening and benevolent image has yielded results. The survey found that 83 per cent of Malaysians and 65 per cent of Indonesians had favourable views of China, a sharp contrast to the findings of a survey five years earlier. The US lagged behind except in the case of the Philippines which continued to be more wary of China. In 2008, however, there was a slight shift in pattern, perhaps consequent to the aggressive actions at sea and another Pu survey found that negative feelings about China in South East Asia had increased. There have been other efforts at use of soft power by China. The largest public demonstration was the 2008 Olympic games. These cost an estimated 70 billion US dollars and were telecast live to 4.7 billion viewers and was used as an opportunity to showcase China's huge economy and its ability to successfully host possibly, the world's biggest event. Its image was buttressed by the grand ceremonies which were choreographed with precision and its impressive medals tally.

Another major effort at the use of soft power has been the launch of the programme to spread Chinese culture and the Chinese language. It was decided to expand soft power through the Confucious Institutes and the first institute was set up in Tashkent in 2004. By 2009 there were 328 Confucious Institutes the world over. The aim is to set up 500 Confucious institutes by 2010 and a 1000 by 2020. China is also focussing on teaching people Chinese and estimates that 40 million people are learning Chinese today throughout the world. In October 2007 the application of soft power by China received a fillip when Chinese President Hu Jintao declared at the 17th Party Congress that China needed to enhance soft power since culture has become a factor of growing significance in the competition in overall national strength. As part of this effort, an amount of 6.6 billion dollars was earmarked for expansion of the media's reach. The result has been the increase in transmissions and transmission time of CCTV channels and China International Radio broadcasts. Two new dailies have been added already; namely, the English and Chinese editions of Global Times as subsidiaries of the party paper People's Daily. The State owned news agency Xinhua has plans to add more than 100 bureaus. China has begun also exhibiting the size of its publishing industry by participating in international book fairs. For example, earlier this year in February it spent 7.5 million dollars in participating in the book exhibition at Frankfurt. Satellite communications are also being expanded with a view to acquiring dominance in the sector of satellite telecommunications and networking activities in the developing world.

Education represents the ideal application of soft power as it directly targets the elite opinion forming segment of a country. It is a long range move. China started targeting this by establishing top flight world class universities and then embarking on programmes promoting student exchanges. It incrementally increased budgetary allocations for education and in 2009 the education budget totals 29 billion dollars. The universities offer Chinese language, medicine, art, culture, etc., courses and scholarships to students to attract them. Today, there are 224,000 overseas students in China and by 2020 China hopes to have over 500,000 overseas students studying in Chinese universities. By way of comparison I may just mention that the US and the UK have about 624,000 and 513,000 overseas students studying in their universities. To achieve the target of 500,000 overseas students China has from this year enhanced the monthly living subsidies for undergraduate overseas students by 50 per cent and similarly for graduate and post graduate students.

But there is still substantial suspicion of China throughout the region and in fact in many parts of the world. This is because the Chinese communist leadership, perhaps, has deep belief that 'power flows from the barrel of a gun', has not eschewed the use of military force and continues to rely heavily on the PLA. Modernisation and strengthening of the PLA has in fact been a consistent theme of the Chinese ambition. The use of force at Tiananmen Square and more recently, to stop Tibetans escaping to Nepal over mountain passes or quell disturbances in Tibet and Xinxiang remind us of another side of China's leadership. Observers noticed that at the prestigious 2008 Olympic games the girl who actually sang the inaugural song was substituted on stage by another because the latter was better looking. Also, a 100,000 PLA personnel were deployed to ensure smooth performances at the games. In the context of Beijing's efforts to allay the apprehensions of countries in the region that China continues to harbour aggressive designs the PLA Navy celebrations held in April 2009 only served to highlight its capabilities. It signalled that the PLA Navy could and is preparing in the future to recover its claims in the off-shore territories.

To conclude, I would paraphrase a remark I heard recently in this very context, "the people of the region listen carefully to the sound of hoof beats of the galloping horsemen of history and are unlikely to forget past Chinese behaviour".

Session II : Discussion

Issue Raised

How can you say that China's soft power undermines international norms, empowers authoritarian regimes like Iran and Korea and lays the foundation for hard power?

Responses

(a) It is agreed that China has contributed to positive international standards and has acted as a responsible stake holder in many cases. However, it has perhaps undermined them through its policy of non-interference in the internal affairs of countries that have low standards for anti-corruption and do not support transparency and accountability in governance. Whereas, if China did not pursue a policy of non-interference, these countries would probably still need to depend on western institutions like the IMF, World Bank etc; which attach reform conditions and minimal conditions for human rights etc.

(b) It is agreed that Chinese performance in the UN Security Council and through 'six party' talks has improved the situation in Iran and Korea. However, since China empowers dictators in places like Sudan and Myanmar, by engaging with them when other countries would not, the net effect is that it is not clear what China's intentions are.

(c) Hard power lays the foundation for soft power because without the looming threat of hard power, China would not be able to exercise its soft power. Soft power in the form of infrastructure investments, development of ports, transportation and roads provide the foundation for setting up future military bases in those areas e.g. the 'string of pearls' theory.

Issue Raised

With the 'Rising China', its economic, military and political power would also grow. In that case, soft power would play a very important role in making China a good stake holder in international affairs. Why is the Chinese leadership not paying adequate attention to soft power and why is it focussed on building up economic strength and military power?

Responses

(a) It stems from the fact that in their priorities, building up of economic power is most important, without which they feel they would not be able to move ahead. To an extent they are correct, because to raise living standards of the people domestically, they do need to have a strong economy. However, what happens is- if while building up of strong economy its orientation is towards having a strong military, it leads to bringing up the whole country to No 1 or No 2 position. In the minds of the Chinese leadership, application of military strength is very important. Hence, soft power becomes number two and is used as an expedient to resolve a situation (temporarily), i.e. to bide time till the mainland China is strong enough to push in and resolve the problem the way they wanted to solve.

(b) Another view was that there was no such thing as soft power. There is only one power and i.e. hard power. It has two components – the economic component and the military component. The economic component is now being made to appear as soft power. It is not soft power. It is projection of Comprehensive National Power. It is the influence of money and military power which is hard power.

Issues Raised

China is reputed to have foreign investment in terms of the US treasury bonds amounting to over One trillion dollars. Sudden liquidation would reverse the value of dollar and progressively bring down the American monetary power. Can China use this power to :

(a) Obtain from the USA various concessions?

(b) Restrict competition in selected areas for China e.g. in African countries?

(c) With the help of the American influence, somehow counter India's growing economic power?

Responses

(a) Firstly, Chinese foreign investments in US dollars amount to more than 1.6 trillion. It is more than that. Holding this kind of reserve is an economic folly. There is no wisdom in doing so. It is like riding a tiger which you cannot get off. China is losing something like $400 billion a year by keeping this money in the US banks because of devaluation (12 per cent last year) and the dollar is likely to devalue further.

(b) China is likely to pay the price for this. In recent history, nations like Iran and Japan have paid for piling reserves in the USA.

(c) Ten years from now, the Chinese reserves would be there. The Americans will then find some other place to buy their goods from. Suddenly, they would show the power of monopsony to China e.g. what happened to baby food, dog food or toxic toys etc? The Chinese boat would be rocked again and again.

(d) A country which intends to rock the USA, ends up being in its clutches. To under estimate and write off the USA is another folly. It is a big industrial power with cutting edge technologies, which makes it a smart power.

(e) China would not be in a position to challenge the power of the USA in the near future. We should not over estimate the role of this 1.6 trillion dollar foreign exchange reserves.

Issue Raised

Is there any chance of negotiated settlement of the border issue between India and China?

Response

The border issue is important. Anne Marie Slaughter, presently Hillary Clinton's Director of Policy in the US State Department has written a major paper on China to say that every time there was economic difficulty within the country, there was a crisis, the country tended to look outwards. Since we have an unfinished problem with China, they would look outwards at us – just like we would do too. We need to be ready to face the problem by taking up confidence building measures, by seeking a state of parity or near parity vis-à-vis China. Our military planners can take a lesson from the fact that whatever happens, one has to be ready and only then can there be peace and stability.

Issues Raised

In the Cold War era, capitalists thought of fighting Communism. What would be the ramifications of the present day economic imbalances vis-à-vis the Chinese investments? How would the current portents play up in the coming decades; say, in the next twenty years?

Response

This is not a fight between democracy and communism. There is no communism in China. China is following an authoritarian form of government. Its inspiration is Lee Kwan Yew. It is not a fight between democracy and totalitarianism. There are two dynamic economies at play in China. China is not going to go the old Soviet Union way. Soviet Union went down, when it was spending 50-55 per cent of its GDP on defence. It had gone totally berserk militarily speaking and did not have the economy to back it up. It was saddled with huge peripheral areas which it had to finance and support. This included Ukraine, Belarus, all the Warsaw Pact Countries, the Commonwealth of Independent States (CIS) Countries. China does not have such a liability. China's economy is pretty homogenous and solid. It is well directed. It has got a huge industrial component. However, it is not in the same league as the USA. The relationship with the USA is not one of equals. It is one of a lower grade economy supplying cheap goods to a high consumptive economy. History seldom repeats itself in that way. What we have is a completely new set of dynamics and China at this moment does not have the wherewithal to compete with the USA and it is unlikely to change, at least not in this Century.

Session II: Chairman's Concluding Remarks

We have had an excellent discussion on the elements of soft power and how China has applied its soft power. Undoubtedly, China's economic performance in the last 20 years has been remarkable. The question arises – Is economics a soft power or is it a clout? As far as China is concerned, it has used its economic strength more as a hard power than as a soft power. Look at the way they have gone about in Africa. The President and the Prime Minister visited Africa and they divided Africa into two, and they offered lots of economic aid to various countries.

Professor Baviera made the point that China has not been that successful in its soft power endeavours as it has been in the other field i.e. economic power play. Mr Mohan Guruswamy has made a seminal point; people outside India do not make this mistake, but in India we tend to believe that somehow China has already overtaken America and that America is in a serious state of decline. Far from it. If the USA's per capita income were to stay absolutely flat at $46,000 and the Chinese were to grow at 7 - 9 per cent and if you applied the rule of 72, 9 years or 8 years to double the per capita income from $3500 to $7000 and $14000 and $28000, it will be 2042 before they catch up with the current American per capita income. That is, as Mohan said, for this Century.

Chinese economic power is important. Its application, its softer roles are problematical because of various reasons. Soft power consists of culture, music and cuisine. In cuisine of course they have an advantage, but their language makes it very difficult for them to export their soft power in its classical sense. That is going to remain in spite of much money being invested in giving scholarships etc. Basically, what has happened is that Deng's advice, *"be humble and bide for your time"* has been forgotten by the Chinese. They are neither humble nor, they are waiting for their time. They are too much in a hurry, and that creates problems.

Professor Baviera described how the Chinese are creating apprehensions in this region. If you see, in spite of the amount of money, etc., which they are investing in Africa, their presence is not liked that much as their benevolence really should call for.

There is a shift of power taking place. As Paul Kennedy brought out in his book "With the collapse of time, the power now resides in Nations' and organisations' hands for a shorter and shorter time", and if the Chinese do not play their cards carefully that moment also will pass. Nonetheless, I do not want to give the impression that there is not something to be applauded about the progress which they have made in such a short time. May be, the typical Chinese wisdom will prevail in the long run and we will have a happier, more equitable and peaceful world.

In the end, I will make one final point, *"You can invest in making a strong nation and you can invest in making a strong state"*. The Soviet Union invested in making a strong State. But a strong nation requires empowering of its people and I think the Chinese have a long way to go. Any authoritarian regime, would have a long way to go to make a strong nation because authoritarian regimes do not empower people; they really limit their creativity and that in the long run does not pay and it gets overtaken.

STRATEGIC CAPABILITY : SPACE,NUCLEAR,POWER PROJECTION AND REGIONAL POWER

THIRD SESSION

Chairman   Rear Admiral KR Menon (Retd)

First Paper   Professor Han Hua , SIS Peking University

Second Paper   Professor Michael Pillsbury, Consultant, USDoD

Third Paper   Mr Yung Sheng Chao, Prospect Foundation, Taipei.

Fourth Paper   Lt Gen (Air Force) Takayoshi Ogawa (Retd),
                   Okazaki Institute, Japan

Fifth Paper   Colonel (now Brigadier) Subodh Kumar,
                   USI Senior Research Fellow

Discussion

Session III : Chairman's Opening Remarks

Rear Admiral K Raja Menon (Retd)

Good morning ladies and gentlemen, and senior citizens of the USI. I must tell you that the continued presence of the older generation is really one of the great strengths of this Institution. You debated some very weighty issues yesterday. The jury is still out on whether the rise is peaceful or not. We are however, sure of one thing that China has certainly risen. To set the background to the discussions this morning, I had a look at some of the great writers on the philosophical culture that defines China. There are some very interesting writings, particularly addressing India. They say things which the world outside does not take seriously, when we use the expression 'harmonious society'. This is a serious concept in China. Under this concept they state, *'we believe in dispute resolution'*. The Chinese say, *'we don't think that disputes should arise if there is a harmonious society'*. Where do we get these ideas from. The Chinese say, *'from this country which they refer to as the western heaven'* - which is supposed to be India. If you were stuck in traffic jam this morning you might not agree that this is *'western heaven'*. But, there it is. When we say China is the 'middle kingdom', they agree but middle kingdom is below western heaven. That also explains why the Chinese get very upset when there is a conflict between Japan and China because they say Japan is a child of this great harmonious society culture. So how could there be a conflict? Now the ones who argue against it and say that there could be conflict because of Marxism. The Chinese say that Marxism is a Western idea and there is nothing

Chinese about Marxism – economic theory of surplus value and all that. After all, it is Mao who said, *'power comes from the barrel of a gun'*.

We have a very learned panel this morning. I will leave maximum time for questions. May I now call upon the first speaker Professor Han Hua from the Beijing University to give her presentation.

Session III : First Paper

Professor Han Hua

If you look at the Nuclear Forces, in the newly released data by the Federation of Association of Scientists of the USA and look at China, you can have a general view about how powerful China has become in terms of strategic capability. In recent years, it is interesting to say there are so many estimates about Chinese Nuclear capability but the figures are gradually getting down. It shows we have 118 Nuclear warheads. Talking about China specifically, another estimate may be a little bit different from this one. It has a total of 275 warheads, which is the highest estimate. If you look specifically at the ICBMs, SLBMs and bombers, you can see that China has developed sufficient Nuclear deterrence capability. People are looking at China's new developments. After seeing the Chinese military parade on the Tiananmen Square a few months ago the people said, China has upgraded its Du Fong missiles – specifically Du Fong 31 and Du Fong 41, and also the Ju Long series of Submarine Launched Ballistic Missiles; and also 033, 034 Nuclear capable Submarines. I would like to share some facets about the Chinese Nuclear build up. Upto 1996 China had done 45 tests. China has a small size trial arsenal, comprising of land, submarine and bombers. We (China) have lesser Nuclear warheads and delivery systems compared with the USA and Russia, and limited 'de- alert status'. It means, the warheads are kept separated from the missiles, and 'slow retaliation' – only one week after the Nuclear attack.

Objective of Chinese Nuclear Strategy is to counter coercion. It means not to yield to Nuclear blackmails and coercion. The western terminology of "deterrence" is neither correct nor accurate word to explain China's strategy. 'Deterrence' translated into Chinese is *wei she* is not an appropriate translation because it is not compatible to 'deterrence', rather it means "coercion". Some Chinese scholars and strategists have already begun to believe in the Western concept of "deterrence". Some Western scholars describe the Chinese Nuclear Strategy as a transformation from 'minimum deterrence' to 'limited deterrence', which signifies their war fighting capability.

What are the differences between "minimum deterrence" and "counter coercion"? The objective of the Chinese nuclear strategy is to counter *'coercion'*. The core strategy is *'no first use'* (NFU) policy. NFU means, 'use only as a last resort'. For China, NFU makes more sense than first use. China's NFU is unconditional. Among the NPT nuclear states China is the only country which concedes to NFU to provide security assurance to nuclear have-nots and nuclear weapon free zones.

China's nuclear modernisation of its Nuclear capability, has three parameters. The first one is, 'increase mobility for survivability', specially for ICBMs and SLBMs. The second direction of the modernisation is 'accuracy'. Smaller warheads make the weapons more accurate. The last one is to change from liquid fuel to solid fuel – to reduce launch preparation time. The rationale of the driving force behind this modernisation, is the vulnerability of Chinese *'limited nuclear deterrence'*. The solid based missiles are vulnerable to attack, solid fuel missiles have higher readiness and low early warning capabilities, low operational capabilities of nuclear submarines. In sum, Chinese vulnerability makes it imperative for China to upgrade its nuclear capability.

The other side of the driving force of Chinese modernisation is China's 'threat perception'. In recent years China has a threat perception from the USA's pre-emptive strike capability and intention. There are two reasons behind this: one is the Nuclear Posture Review in 2001 and the other is an article: "The End of MAD – US Nuclear Primacy" published in the Foreign

Affairs Journal. These two developments in the US really made the Chinese feel not very confident when they talk about their nuclear capability. Another driving force is 'The US Missile Defence'. The third one is, the Chinese apprehension from the US intent for use of nuclear weapons. More US nuclear weapons are targeting China and there are more US nuclear submarines in the Pacific Ocean.

Overall, if you look at the newly published 2009 White Paper in China you can have more concrete views about Chinese nuclear strategy. The White Paper says, "China is committed to the NFU" of nuclear weapons. China also made an assurance to Rumsfeld, the Secretary of Defence of the USA when he visited China four years ago. The Chinese military strategy "Calls for the building of a lean but effective deterrence force and the flexible use of different means of deterrence". China has also made a more clear statement about their different strategies. For example, "During peacetime nuclear weapons don't target any country, but in crisis nuclear forces go into a state of alert, and when facing nuclear attack second artillery will get ready for a nuclear counter attack to deter the enemy from using nuclear weapons against China".

China has developed small size and sufficient nuclear capability. China's nuclear development has been slow and China has a unique strategy of countering coercion. About new directions of Chinese nuclear future, we can say that China is trying to retain or upgrade counter-coercion capability that includes :

(a) The counter measures to US Missile Defence System

(b) Survivability of a nuclear first strike

(c) NFU will be kept as the core of the strategy.

Actually in recent years, specifically after the US raised the 'Missile Defence Plan; in China, especially, in the Arms Control community we have a big debate about whether China should keep the NFU policy intact or they should change it into some conditional NFU.

In the end, the mainstream in China's security community still believes that NFU serves Chinese interest the most.

Lastly, nuclear disarmament, so far we have signed the agreement reached by the USA and Russia but since Obama proposed the 'Nuclear Weapons Free World Plan' and China has been asked or pressurised to have something to do in the 'Nuclear Disarmament' field; in general China takes a positive view about Nuclear Weapons Free Zone but we still think the two nuclear powers ought to take the lead to dramatically reduce the number of the warheads and the delivery systems. The quality of weapons also matter. They have to do something before China is drawn in the process.

Chairman's Remarks

The professor has given a very powerful message. We have to take note from all sources that are available to us that the number of nuclear warheads that China is attempting to stabilise at, is considerably lower than what its financial capacity is capable of sustaining. Whether it is 275 or 300 or 350, it is around that – which is a very positive step. In our part of the world, we are a little more concerned with the proliferation to Pakistan which is certainly an issue that might come around to bite them, considering the present political turmoil in Pakistan. The other issue that we have to take note of is what China has a very large number of non-nuclear tipped ballistic missiles. How does the surveillance system tell the difference when one of these missiles is launched as to whether the tip is nuclear or non-nuclear?

Session III : Second Paper

Professor Michael Pillsbury

The 'six questions' up for discussion are extremely important. There are two big obstacles to answering these questions. First is Chinese soft power, affecting the thinking of military planners. During our conference yesterday and again this morning apologies are being made for military planning. The idea seems to be that we all want peace; my country wants peace, China wants peace, therefore we should not think about worst case scenarios. The problem with that is that if you look at the 'memoirs' in India about 1962, on our side and on the Indian side, you find tragic efforts in the 1950s to do just this kind of thinking. Then you find at the moment of Chinese attack, your Prime Minister in desperation asking for US air force units to be called in to defend India because there were no forces left between Calcutta and the Chinese military frontline.

You cannot invent 'A Force One Commando' in just one day. You cannot have signals intelligence, anti-terrorism measures to prevent what happened in Mumbai. It is the same thing with China. We all want peace with China. I believe Professor Han Hua was giving American views. She very carefully quoted American left wing pro-China views of China's nuclear forces. I hope that is true. I hope the Chinese do not follow the model of the Soviet Union and try to match the USA with 10,000 warheads. But when the US President asked China's President on April 20, 2006: Can we please have a dialogue between our Strategic Forces Commanders? The Chinese President said, "Yes, good idea." It was announced by the White House publicly that same day. It has never happened. The Chinese Nuclear

Forces Commander always has some place else to visit. He has been to Argentina, Chile and many other places. He just cannot quite come to the US Strategic Forces Command. Most recently, our Chinese highest level visitor went out there, and really had nothing to say. He brought the Second Artillery – Professor Han Hua just mentioned. He brought the Political Commissar because this man would know little bit about the Chinese future Nuclear planning. No, he had nothing to say. So, we have to use American left wing pro-China statistics, and comments from the Chinese Defence White Paper on a topic of extreme importance. Where is the Chinese Nuclear force going in 20 years? An important thing for all of these six questions is: How much money will China have to spend? There is a Rand Corporation study online, done a few years ago that estimates the Chinese Navy budget, cumulative: How much money will they have to spend from year 2005 to 2025? Over those 20 years they have 500 billion dollars to spend. Rand estimates appear conservative. It could be much more. The Rand estimated that the Chinese air Force would have 500 billion dollars cumulative to spend, that is a lot of money.

Look at the low level scenario. A world of peace – China has great trust in American military deployments that are not aimed at China, does not see India as a threat, does not see Japan as a threat, then this level of money could be spent on very internally focussed systems for China – self defence. There is a list of about 25 subjects where China talks about (in a book I wrote 10 years ago) internal self defence needs. China has no early warning system for its nuclear forces for example. Spend a lot of money on that. China is very concerned about the island chains opposite China's coast, a few hundred miles out that some kind of foreign enemy could fortify these island chains and blockade China. If I missed a lot in Chinese military writings they can spend a lot of money on that over the next 20 years or they can spend nothing. Here no island chain blockade will happen. Their main topic was Japan when they raised this question. Thirdly, they have a fear of India. They see an Indian threat and they write about it. They can spend a lot of money on the Indian threat or nothing. So, if you look at our questions, the area of strategic reach; should they attempt to protect their sea lanes of communication (SLOC) coming to the Indian Ocean. A lot of Chinese military authors say-yes this is a threat. But suppose Indian soft power reassures China, no we have no intention of making the Indian Ocean an 'Indian' Ocean. We will never interfere with Chinese oil tankers coming through here and we do not care if China forms military agreements with Burma or Pakistan, and other places, we do not care, we will do nothing about this. If Indian soft power succeeds, China could spend nothing on power projection, strategic reach in the Indian Ocean or they could have a trillion dollars to spend on it over the next 20 years for the Air Force and Navy, cumulative acquisition budgets combined. These Rand estimates are weapons acquisition budgets only.

A look at the Assasin's Mace concept. Professor Han Hua made a very good point that China has a unique strategic culture and approach to many strategic problems. The Americans have a hard time in understanding this term. It seems to mean, one Chinese General told me, when I asked him: What is this Assassin's Mace? I have to translate this for my books. How do you put it, he said, very easy Dr Pillsbury. You see James Bond movies – at the very end, James Bond always has a very special piece of technology he can pull out of his briefcase or somewhere and he saves the situation. He was going to be killed but he saves himself because he has what the Chinese call Assassin's Mace. This is a 1200 years old concept from Tang Dynasty – it is brought out secretly. It is not known to the enemy. So, you can have a conference topic on what is China's Assassin's Mace? It is secret. But it is a war winning concept. You build the technology and then you use it at the time to save yourself from disaster. A number of Chinese military officers have discussed the Assassin's Mace concept indiscreetly. While some Americans have written about this, the Chinese civilian scholars make fun of it. They said no, no, no – 'Assassins Mace' just means a kick-ass weapon. It is just a colloquial expression. For example, while dating a girl, the Chinese might use a special technique that may be unique – not used before by anyone else. Your Department of Defence (DoD) people are just wasting their time. There is no such thing. Chinese soft power can be very effective at putting people to sleep.

The other concepts. Professor Han Hua did a very good job on the low end nuclear missile modernisation. She made a very important point. American developments, and perhaps Indian and Japanese, make a huge difference on what the Chinese would do with their own missile forces. In America if you look back at the 1980s, 1990-91 public comments about Chinese missile forces, over the next 20 years, i.e. around 2000-2001, guess, how many people would have forecast that China would deploy more than 1000 short range missiles against Taiwan? It did happen. Nobody projected a short range ballistic missile build up opposite Taiwan means that the US policy and Taiwan policy had no chance to work on heading off or persuading China please do not do this. The intelligence community failed so badly in the forecasts in 1980's and in 1990 that the opportunity for policy makers to do something was taken away. Chinese soft power and self deception by American analysts was very strong. In terms of integrated joint war capability, what is the main conclusion all experts on Chinese military draw in the USA? If you read through all our studies, what you will find is: China is very bad at integrated joint warfare capability. They cannot do this, very backward, no hope, trying hard in their training scenarios but very pathetic. If that is right, we have the low end scenario for military planners. But there is a wonderful book in Chinese which I hope someone would translate. It is called Science of Joint Campaign Training. It is written by a Chinese General who is Chief of Operations. His name is Shu Gan Fu. This book gives 24 Campaign Plans on military operations that, 'training should be done now, for the future'. Of the 24 Campaign Plans, all of them are 'Integrated Joint Campaign' scenarios. For example, 'Island Chain Blockade' says – Second Artillery Missile Forces, PLA Air force, PLA Navy, and other units must cooperate, and describes how this can be done. Will they have any success in doing this? If Chinese soft power is successful, the American answer and the Indian answer will be no. China cannot make any progress in this area and so our military planners should not plan for it. That seems to be the current situation.

China has numerous requests to the USA and some to India. You have to think about Chinese soft power in terms of these requests:-

(a) Number one, the DoD Annual Report on Chinese military power: very detailed, 60 pages, on line, lot of graphics. The best effort of the DoD to understand China today, because of request from Congress. It is a Law, it must be done. China says cancel this Law. Do not do it anymore, as this Report is very misleading. It upsets people and in a way it blocks the effort of Chinese soft power to claim peaceful rise, so don't do this.

(b) Number two, stop your pressure on Europe and Israel who want to sell weapons to China worth billions of dollars.

(c) Number three, do not sell weapons to India. This would be very unharmonious world, especially anything that helps India to upgrade maritime patrol capability in the Indian Ocean or anything that helps India along the frontier.

(d) Another Chinese request – Arunachal Pradesh should be returned to China, Aksai Chin Tibetan Plateau area is Chinese territory. In the US mapping it is always shown contested territory with little blue lines in Aksai Chin Area and also in Arunachal Pradesh. Chinese friends object to this: Why does Pentagon do this? This is Chinese territory. Also, India maintains a government in exile for Tibet; Dalai Lama's position is: My government, my parliament, my cabinet ministers must return to Lhasa. This is the topic of dialogue China would not have. Why does India do this, why does America seem to passively consent this?

(e) Another request from China, cancel the limits. There are 12 legally required limits about topics that the US military cannot discuss with China; nuclear deterrence, power projection, logistics etc. The US Congress passed a law 10 years ago which says, you are going too far in military talks with China, you must never talk about these 12 things. China says this law must be repealed. The US would not sell spare parts of weapons we sold to China in the 1980s. China says you (America) must do this.

Chinese soft power includes a number of demands. I have only mentioned a few of them. If you really want soft power to succeed, not only should there be no military planning against high end contingencies involving China; but, America and India must make specific moves to bring about a harmonious world.

The views expressed by me are personal and do not represent the US government in any way. I hope our efforts to use American soft power towards China will succeed because our view is: China needs to follow Confucius tradition, needs to defend its internal issues only, needs to avoid these six areas, needs to be more transparent about its own military build up in the next 10 or 20 years with specific figures – not relying on Union of Scientists and other Left Wing US organisations. We have a long list of American soft power hopes for a Chinese approach to a harmonious world and hope American soft power will succeed as well as Chinese soft power does.

Chairman's Remarks

It is not surprising that in a military institution we may think that soft power is not valid, but if any of you got frightened this morning as I did when Michael was speaking; well, that is soft power, to get you frightened without hitting you on the head. He made a very valid point. It is $ 500 billion that is going to be available for the PLA at 37 per cent of the budget for the next 25 years. If this is not going to be used to build up a giant Navy- how else is it going to be used? This is a challenge for the Chinese diplomacy to tell the world that either they are not going to spend that much money or they are going to spend it on something else. There is this challenge in trying to tell the Chinese - do not build up in the Indian Ocean. The shadow boxing that is going to happen should take strategic directions more clearly.

Session III : Third Paper

Mr Yung Sheng Chao

My presentation will cover PRC's military force projection capability and regional security.

China held its 60th Anniversary parade last month. The PLA displayed most updated weapons systems of its different services. The weapons display revealed transition of strategic gravity of the PLA from 'Homeland Defence' to assuring the "Stability of China's Land and Maritime Periphery'. To meet its energy needs, China would be highly dependent on crude oil produced in the Persian Gulf. The proportion of imports by the sea lanes of communication (SLOC) will be more and more. This has also resulted in development of major weaknesses in China's Strategic Forces. Many Chinese writers recognise the potential vulnerability of China's SLOC. Therefore, the need to establish control of the Indian Ocean Region (IOR), South China Sea, maritime transport routes and expansion of influence of military power on the first island chain has become an inevitable choice of China.

What is China's approach? China's approach to deal with this challenge appears to be reflected in sustained effort to develop the capability to 'attack' long range military force that might deploy or operate within the Western Pacific area. In this context, China envisages anti-access and aerial denial power increasingly; providing multiple layers of offensive systems utilising the sea air space and cyber space. The PLA is also organising Second Artillery, new generation aircraft and ships to engage and for repelling a foreign aggression. The US Department of Defence

(DoD) 2009 estimates that China will take until the end of this decade or longer to produce a model force capable of defeating a moderate size adversary. Meanwhile, China will not be able to project and sustain small military units far beyond China before 2015 and would not be able to project and sustain large force in combat operations far from China until the following decade.

What most people are concerned about is the establishment of China's 'anti-access' operational capability. In China Military Report 2009, the US DoD points out that the PLA hopes to build integrated systems in the 21st Century based on anti-ship ballistic missiles, global positioning and tracking systems, C4ISR systems and inter-continental ballistic missile guidance system to tackle enemy surface ships. China believes that in modern warfare, because their logistics and mobility are relatively weak, they would use short range and medium range ballistic missiles; like the Dong Fong 15, land attack cruise missiles, special forces as well as computer network attacks to deter or prevent the involvement of any third country in its interests. The PLA, firstly, tried to refuse access, but could not persuade the US defence research community to either agree or comply. Thereafter, it decided not to compete with the US warships and fighter jets; but to aim at preventing development of US military capability, of operating freely around the coastal areas in China. Over the last decade, the PLA has made great progress in this field. The range of its conventional ballistic missile and cruise missiles can cover most of the US military bases in East Asia. At the same time, the PLA is also building satellite-short base radar and other sensors monitoring network consisting of integrated systems to locate and track enemy's surface warships, hundreds of kilometres away from its coastal areas.

China's combat operations efforts in recent years reflect their intent to engage in multilayer interceptions. The first problem in implementing this strategy is 'detecting the US aircraft carriers'. Research literature on the PLA's anti-aircraft carrier operations emphasise the importance of

C4ISR network data link. Many Chinese military scholars believe that detection of the US aircraft carrier battle groups is not a problem. China has been developing and applying ocean reconnaissance satellites. After this C4ISR systems are put into service, the detection range for locating aircraft carriers can be greatly enhanced, enabling the PLA to project its softer combat power to outer waters 300-500 km from the shore. In the new round of arms procurement from Russia, China has been paying great attention towards integration of C4ISR with data link. Whilst Russia's 82N data link technology is transferred to the Chinese force, the combat platform will have a much enhanced capability in conducting integrated anti-aircraft carrier operations.

The Chinese plan to conduct anti-access tactics against aircraft carriers successfully, comprises of three different layers. Within the outer range of 2000km from the Chinese coast line – known as the 'outer layer', the PLA will use tactical missiles. The weapons systems used could include the DF21 series, DF15 Model II and the Zero Night series submarines to deter an adversary. The 'second layer' of the deterrence covers the range from 1500-1000km. The main weapon systems to cover this range include K-36 Sub with superior concealed features, SU-30 fighters and JH7. The 'third layer' covers the range from 500-200km. It is connected by including many platforms like 956-M, 052 Class DDGs and short range ballistic missiles.

It is stressed that the Americans 'using the costly aircraft carriers' is the key to their global power projection capability. However, in the future, the Chinese anti-access strategy would face crisis; i.e. when the USA decides to pull back their aircraft carriers far away from China's coast. They would then be beyond the effective range of the Chinese aircraft. This would reduce their capability to provide air cover for the US front, or capability to conduct strikes against them from land and sea. In addition to this more direct mode of attack, China is experimenting with anti-satellite weapons and techniques for striking down enemy's computer networks;

thereby making them 'deaf and blind' during the critical opening phase of a war. China's international behaviour is driven by a long standing ambition to see China play a role of a great power in East Asia and globally. In other words, its goal is not only Taiwan, it is even beyond that, hoping to play an important role in the Asia-Pacific region and even the whole world.

What is the impact of this play on the region? China is gradually changing the 'regional stability' and 'military balance' in East Asia and South Asia. At present China's military deployment beyond Taiwan is focused on areas extending to Central Asia, South Asia and the Korean Peninsula – also the South China Sea waterways. In Central Asia, the PLA tends to cooperate with countries to implement the 'National Anti-terrorism Mission' and to jointly protect the oil and gas resources. In South Asia, it is planning to use ground troops, armed police, navy and the air force and the missile forces to deal with India and strengthening military cooperation with Pakistan and Burma. To consolidate it's 'capabilities and activities' in South Asia and North Asia, the PLA would face confrontation from South Korea, Japan, the USA and Russia. China also needs to pay close attention to whether the situation in North Korea could lead to clashes in the region.

China's rapid military modernisation, which has improved the PLA ground force operational capability considerably, has been the most ignored one by the world in the past 30 years. It has produced great pressures on present day land neighbours. Due to recently developed armoured vehicles, the PLA can mobilise its troops rapidly by rail and highways system which have been constructed very speedily in the last decade. From the Chinese perspective China today is a geopolitical land power state. Historically also China had always performed the role of a strong land power. Predictably, China cannot build its naval capabilities superior to the US Navy in the near future. It is too unrealistic technically for China to use its middle sized aircraft carrier fleet to protect its oil transportation SLOC, which cover a distance of 7000 km, i.e. if the USA and India become China's rivals. China understands the situation very well that the PLA Navy would not be able to compete with the American and Indian Navies in the Indian Ocean. Therefore, it must extend its land power to its South Western periphery and utilise land power supremacy to offset its sea power inferiority in South Asia. During the process of military power transition, China behaved carefully to hide its land power strategic intention to serve the purpose of not provoking the 'China threat suspicion' amongst other countries, especially its neighbours.

The Chinese have been successful in guiding the focus of outside world to its naval development and to influence the Western observers to analyse the possible outcomes of this development. Scholars continue to debate, without consensus about the strategic intentions behind the recent development of the PLA Navy. China has reshaped its outdated ground forces step by step and transformed them into a modern force – both in quality and quantity. In the naval area, the achievements have made the PLA Navy capable of sailing into the blue ocean.

Based on rapid modernisation, China's military has made significant advances. It has enabled the PLA to extend its power into China's land and maritime periphery. Due to lack of transparency in China's military modernisation, the improvement of PLA's warfare capability would only create more security pressures and suspicion amongst all its neighbours. The continued improvement in China's economy will certainly translate into further enhancement in its military capability. The sharp increase in the military forces of China is an indisputable fact. Their anti-access strategy training, even without a war, will cause a deterrent effect on neighbouring countries in this region, including the USA. Of course, construction of Chinese military power should not necessarily mean that it would lead to conflict.

History, however, reminds us that expansion of military prowess results in conflicts only. This is the process of countries growing and developing strategic capabilities for obtaining more benefits for themselves. China cannot avoid it. The USA and other Asia Pacific countries would also have to face it in the future.

Chairman's Remarks

Thank you Mr Yung Sheng Chao. Living in Taiwan, and realising the fact that China's soft power is not succeeding in its projections, of convincing its neighbours that its rise is peaceful, must be disturbing. We have to understand this: *'spending of the huge amount of money, which is available to China, is not going to cause threatening power projection capabilities'* - that is a serious challenge. Of course, the Chinese would probably say, that an 'anti-access' strategy for them is 'defensive' but for the Taiwanese it is clearly 'offensive'. So, there is a strategic gap here.

The two issues which have been brought up, are the ones about which the countries on the periphery are aware. Firstly, China appears to be working on trying to win the pre-hostilities escalation phase by denying space assets to a competing power; and the other of course is 'identifying the *'Assassin's Mace'*. Is it the Radar, or Infra Red terminal homing of ballistic missiles, backed by Over the Head Radars. We assume that this is coming. If it is, then it is going to change the nature of Maritime Warfare.

Session III : Fourth Paper

Lieutenant General (Air Force) Takayoshi Ogawa (Retd)

The focus of the talk will be on 'Chinese Space Warfare Capability'. Firstly, the Chinese Space capability developments are very confidential. Today, many of the technological advances have broadened the Space capability into commercial and military areas. Our social infrastructure would collapse completely without space capabilities. In military application, space capabilities are essential, both in strategic and in tactical operations. Even in early 1991, during Operation Desert Storm in Iraq, space enabled a wide range of capabilities to the US and coalition forces; which included missile warning, communications, lasers, surveillance and reconnaissance. Space forces are now closely embedded in combat operations and play a key role in providing data surveillance, reach and power for the nation's civilian and military radars, e.g. Global Positioning System (GPS) navigation and timing signal has enabled to turn 'dumb bomb' into 'smart munitions' effectively with relatively little cost. Satellite Communication (SATCOM) also plays a major role in feeding data information to the 21st Century military, connecting decision makers and combat forces across the globe. SATCOM enables information sharing at all levels of warfare. For instance, Space enabled communications link transfers a lot of information including threat data, intelligence information and tasking orders.

China is one of the most active Space power in Asia. It has been investing in Space capabilities since the 1960s. Its Space programme was partially shielded from interference during the cultural revolution in early 1970s, when many other programmes faced severe disruption. The investment has paid off for China. It has resulted in visible enhancement of its 'prestige'. China used its Space programme to announce its great power status and regional dominance. China's President Hu Jintao described the success of Shenzhou – 5, which was the first Chinese manned spaceship in October 2003, as a historic step taken by the Chinese people in their endeavour to surmount the peak of the world science and technology. The motives that guide both Chinese civil and military Space efforts fall into three categories. The first involves China in bringing Space capabilities equivalent with other developed nations. Furthermore, China intended to show its prowess as a super power. China also hopes to take advantage of new technologies like Micro Satellites to create new Space capabilities that would also allow it to exceed developed nations.

China looks to these new technologies to provide asymmetric advantages against the United States and other potential opponents. This means that military Space architecture for China looked very different from that used by the USA or Russia. It means not a true multiplier of weapons systems but a symbolic status of technologies. So, China also wants Space to provide these eye-catching activities which enhance Chinese prestige and influence. Chinese activities in Space were undertaken primarily to affirm or enhance prestige and influence rather than continuously building up operational capabilities so far. The long term goal is to make Space operations integral part of China's national power.

Chinese manned orbital mission is a part of its ambitious programme for exploration. The next phase of the manned programme was Shenzhou-7 launched in September 2008. Shenzhou-7 carried three astronauts and one of those astronauts carried out a Space walk. Between 2010 and 2012 there will be a docking manoeuvre with another Spacecraft followed by a construction of the permanent Space station – establishment of a permanent Space station is the major goal of the manned Space programme.

China has another Space project, working on unmanned Lunar Exploration programme named Changai. The Lunar programme has three phases, planned over the next 12 years. Changai-I was launched successfully in October 2007, took Moon's surface pictures and is now still orbiting the Moon. China hopes that success of the Changai project will set the stage for manned Lunar missions. China's Space budget was secret until 1994. It has still not been made public. It was estimated to be between $1 to $3 billion per year. This includes both military and civilian Space projects, but this does not include all Space related expenditure. One US specialist estimates that China spends a little less than one half of one per cent of the GDP for all the Space programmes. Since the GDP of China is growing rapidly, this may mean that the Space budget will increase every year.

Chinese Space related technologies are notable e.g. take their capabilities in remote sensing. Remote sensing technologies are a vital element of information technologies. Chinese military has identified them as a vital area for building Space capabilities. China has built and flown numerous remote sensing and reconnaissance satellites. The first Chinese model was primitive having poor image resolution. Overtime, Chinese remote sensing effort has become more sophisticated and improved.

The most visible example of current Chinese military Space programme is the Anti Satellite (ASAT) test. The guided laser ASAT weapon that China tested in January 2007 appears to be part of a larger effort to deploy a range of ASAT capabilities. There are press reports that China is also developing other kinds of ASAT weapons including ground based lasers and jammers against satellite signals. The ASAT test involves direct delivery system to intercept a ballistic missile or a satellite. The Chinese intentions for the test may be to confirm its Asymmetric Warfare capabilities against the USA and to show its Space hegemony in this region. Perhaps the most interesting thing about the test was that China miscalculated the reaction to it. They did not expect global condemnation of their ASAT test which caused Space debris. This miscalculation reflects inexperience in international politics and a certain degree of hubris found in China's economic success. Anyway, if China deploys ASAT weapons it would hold satellites in the global orbit at risk. Those geo Space assets would significantly affect most military operations. They would pose a special potential threat to the US military operations in the Pacific; which would also include US responses, in case of Taiwan contingency.

A view of what China has built and launched suggests that China's military Space effort is intended primarily to demonstrate technology and to test many different types of satellites. China has built almost a full range of military Space capabilities and it could rapidly deploy satellites for signalling, intelligence, reconnaissance, geo-navigation and other services. If China has not yet done so, does not mean that it will not do so in the future. The civil Space programme seems to be the high priority for now, but China is clearly focussed on military use of Space for asymmetric approaches to conflict. Despite a range of potential responses, no single option is either simple and cheap or one that would work fully and effectively.

Chairman's Remarks

Thank you General. There is enough study going on here in India too, to recognise that the Space is a new frontier. Just as the 'seas' were the new frontier in the 15th Century and if you have failed in the challenge like we failed in the 15th century, then you would also get colonised. But, one of the unfortunate aspects is that Space scientists have a very close access to political leaders, who actually eventually handout the budgets. Although politicians may not understand rocket science, they are very quick to understand that successful Space programmes, particularly putting a man on the Moon actually helps to win domestic elections. It even makes the stock markets go up!

Session III : Fifth Paper

Brigadier Subodh Kumar

Chinese Space Warfare Capabilities
How can China be Expected to use her Demonstrated Space Warfare Capability?

Introduction

China is today the undisputed space super-power of Asia and the fastest rising star in the hierarchy of the extant space powers. Supported by a fast growing GDP and a large military-industrial complex, China has one of the most ambitious space programmes of world. Over the years, in addition to the large family of Long March series of space launch vehicles, China has a developed a variety of satellites and space applications spanning the entire spectrum of space activities. China is the third nation to have successfully achieved manned spaceflight following the USA and the erstwhile USSR. It may well soon be the second to land a man on the Moon, a fact now begrudgingly recognised by US space experts. In fact, in Sep 2007, Michael Griffin, the then Chief NASA administrator is reported to have said, "I personally believe that China will be back on the moon before we are. I think when that happens, Americans will not like it. But they will just have to not like it".

While the multifaceted and rapid growth of Chinese space capabilities is being keenly observed by the entire world, what is perhaps more significant from the Indian perspective is that most analysts agree that the one defining characteristic of the Chinese space programme is its military orientation. As the international consortium Space Security Index 2009 puts it – "China's governmental space program does not maintain a strong separation between civil and military applications." Even today a large chunk of Chinese satellites are either pure military or dual-use, launched and operated by state-owned military industrial corporations. China is one of the few nations with a proven offensive space warfare capability. China has a large number of military oriented communication, navigation and remote-sensing satellites in orbit and is perhaps the third largest user of military satellites outside US and Russia. It is also noteworthy that China has known capability to launch electronic intelligence (ELINT) and electronic warfare (EW) satellites. China is also in the process of setting up a sophisticated satellite based Qu Dian C4I system broadly modelled on the US Joint Tactical Information Distribution System (JTIDS). However in what may be called the crowning glory of the Chinese space warfare capabilities, China became the third country in the world with a demonstrated anti-satellite (ASAT) capability after the successful destruction of a satellite with a ground based interceptor in Jan 2007. It can thus be stated unequivocally that *space power forms an important part of the Chinese Revolution in Military Affairs (RMA).*

India, on the other hand, while being an aspiring space power with an ambitious space programme, is a relative newbie in the field of military uses of outer space. Most Indian achievements in space have primarily been in civilian commercial or scientific fields. While the Indian space programme is globally acclaimed and the Indian space establishment has consistently proven that it can match the best in capabilities and innovation, the reality is that India lags far behind in space warfare capabilities and has much ground to cover before it can fully leverage its space prowess to enhance its national security, project its military power, and safeguard its national interests. This capability gap, especially in relation to China, unless urgently addressed, cannot but be detrimental to India's security. It is in this context that the Chinese space warfare capabilities and philosophy are of a special interest to India. However before discussing the Chinese space capabilities in detail, a few issues related to the geopolitical significance of outer space forcing more and more countries to seek space capabilities driving need to be highlighted.

Geopolitical Significance of Space

Clash of Interests

The 21st century will undoubtedly witness an exponential increase in space activities by an increasing number of players. Mankind seems to be at the cusp of a vigorous military and economic exploitation of outer space and perhaps prove true the prophetic words of the visionary Russian space engineer Konstantin Tsiolkovsky who had predicted as early as 1903 - *"Mankind will not remain forever on earth, but, in a quest for light and space, will first timidly penetrate the atmosphere and later conquer the whole of the solar system"*. History bears witness that whenever military and economic interests of nations have clashed, on land, sea or air it has invariably led to a struggle for control and at times, war. There is no reason to presume a future outer space rivalry will produce different results. Therefore, it would be safe to assume that space exploitation and domination will form an important component of contemporary and future military strategy. Hence a focus on developing space capabilities forms a crucial component of the grand strategy of all major powers. China is no different and considers space activities *as a key component of its overall development strategy and a major contributor to its Comprehensive National Power.*

Duality of Space Assets

Another factor which enhances the geopolitical significance of space is the inherent duality of space assets. Though all nations profess to pursue space activities for 'peaceful purposes' and 'for benefit of mankind', the fact of the matter are that by their very nature, space activities are innately dual-use. For example, there is not much difference between a ballistic missile and a space launch vehicle. In fact the first lot of space launch vehicles developed by the United States, Russia and China were direct derivatives of ballistic missiles. The first Soviet satellite, Sputnik-1 was launched by a modified R-7 ICBM, and the first American satellite, Explorer-1 was launched by a Jupiter-C rocket derived from the Redstone ICBM. Even the first Chinese satellite, the DFH-1 was launched by the Long March-1 rocket, a direct derivative of the DF-1 ICBM. In a similar vein, it is easy to envisage that remote sensing satellites can also be used for military intelligence, surveillance and reconnaissance (ISR) and telecommunication satellites for military communications. Perhaps one of the most obvious recent example of this duality is the widespread use of Global Positioning System satellites for military targeting and guidance. *Thus given the inherent dual-use capability of space systems, it would not be incorrect to state that even a 'purely' civilian space programme would have some military spin-offs and a considerable deterrent value.*

Increase in the Number of Space Players

It is perhaps due to the dual-use capabilities of space assets that more and more nations are clamouring to join the 'Space Club'. Today there are nine nations with demonstrated space launch capabilities. These are US, Russia, European Union (France and UK have launched satellites independently before formation of EU), Japan, India, Israel and Iran. Many other countries are waiting-in-the-wings with active space programmes in varying stages of development. These include North Korea, South Korea, Brazil, Ukraine, Romania, Indonesia, Australia, Kazakhstan, Taiwan, Pakistan, Azerbaijan, Turkey, Malaysia, New Zealand, South Africa, and Canada. In addition to these, there are a number of nations who have restrained their developmental efforts to satellites and satellite applications while relying on commercial launch facilities of other nations. It is thus easy to conjecture that the future will see a dramatic rise in space-enabled nations.

With so many players, some not on best of terms, it is that doubtful that space will remain unaffected by global and regional events. It is perhaps inevitable that terrestrial rivalries will sooner or later spill over to space thus raising fears that outer space may well become the battle ground for geopolitics in the 21st century. It is also noteworthy that while the Outer Space Treaty 1967 prohibits placing of nuclear weapons or WMD in space, other military uses are not expressly prohibited. It is evident that the framework of international space law, at least in its present form, is inadequate to prevent further militarisation of space. Even in the unlikely eventuality of most future space powers pursuing a primarily civilian space programme, it would still be safe to assume that they would divert at least some portion of their space resources for military purposes for enhancing their national security. In this context it is noteworthy that even small countries like Greece and Belgium are active participants along with Spain and Italy in the Helios very-high-resolution optical imaging military reconnaissance programme led by France. The first satellite Helios 2A was launched in 2004 and the second Helios 2B in 2009. *It can thus be asserted with a fair amount of certainty that with the increase in the number of space players, militarization of space is only likely to increase in the future.*

Missile Proliferation and Space Militarisation

Closely linked to the issue of space militarisation is the issue of missile proliferation. It is well known that an Intercontinental Ballistic Missile and a Space Launch Vehicle are essentially similar. The first space launch vehicles developed by US, Soviet Union, China and United Kingdom were derivatives of ballistic missiles which themselves evolved from German rockets of World War II. Therefore, any nation with ballistic missile capability has an inherent potential of developing space launch capabilities. Recent examples include Iran's *Safir2* SLV which is reported to be a derivative of its *Shahab 3B* missile which itself is a derivative of North Korean *Nodong* missile. *It is thus quite obvious that missile proliferation directly or indirectly contributes to militarization of space.*

In this context China's record of missile proliferation leaves much to be desired. In fact the famous Cox report submitted by a Select Committee of the US House of Representatives does not mince any words in pointing an accusing finger at China and openly alleges that "The PRC has transferred ballistic missile technology to Iran, Pakistan, North Korea, Saudi Arabia, Libya and other countries". That most of the 'client' Chinese states are slowly but steadily migrating from ballistic missile to space capabilities raises justifiable fears of use or misuse of missile proliferation and space capability as a tool for 'containment'.

Sino-Indian Space Equation

Evolutionary Overview

Perhaps the military orientation of the Chinese space programme and the lack thereof in case of India can be traced to the evolutionary trajectory followed by two space programmes. While the roots of Chinese space programme lie in her attempts to develop ballistic missiles with Russian help in the 1950-60's, the Indian space programme was started in the 1960's purely for scientific and civilian purposes. Following the example of the US and the USSR, China focused on a parallel development of ballistic missiles, space launch vehicle capabilities and manned space flight. The first Chinese ballistic missile *Dong Feng-1 (DF-1)* or *East Wind-1* was launched successfully on in 1960. The first satellite *Dong Fang Hong-1 (DFH-1)* or *The East is Red* was launched in 1970 using a *Chang Zheng-1 (CZ-1)* or *Long March-1* rocket (basically a modified version of *Dong Feng-4* ballistic missile). India on the other concentrated its energies in satellite development and later migrated to space launch vehicles. The first Indian satellite *Aryabhata* was launched in 1975 using a Soviet launch vehicle. It was only in 1980 that India succeeded in placing a *Rohini* experimental satellite in orbit using the indigenous SLV-3 rocket. The first Indian ballistic missile was to come as late as 1988. This difference in their histories was to set the tone for the future development of the space programmes. Even today most analysts consider China to be way ahead of India in the space launch vehicle technology. India on the other hand is considered to have a slight edge over China in communication and remote-sensing satellite technology.

A rather interesting aspect of the early years of the Chinese space programme is the life story of its founding father and first director; Tsien Hsue Shen who orchestrated both the missile and space programmes till his retirement in 1991. An expatriate from US, he was one of the co-founders of the renowned Jet Propulsion Laboratory (JPL) and an important member of the American ballistic missile programme. He was even given the honorary rank of a Colonel in the USAF and was a part of the team which entered Germany at the end of World War II to locate and bring back key personnel and documents of the German rocket programme. The team was successful in its mission and brought back many Nazi rocket scientists including the celebrated Wernher von Braun. Fortuitously for the Chinese, Tsien was victimised during the McCarthy era and accused of being a communist. Eventually his security clearance was stripped off and he was forced to leave the US. China welcomed him with open arms, hailed him as a hero, and promptly made him in charge of the ballistic missile and space programmes. Not only did Tsien bring the latest knowledge, best practices and techniques from the US, but he was also successful in negotiating the 1956 agreement on transfer of nuclear and rocket technology with Russia, including training of Chinese students in Russian universities. The Chinese space programme thus had the benefit of American expertise, Soviet assistance and backing of the powerful PLA in the crucial formative years.

These historical factors ensured that the Chinese space establishment and the PLA maintained strong links which have endured till date. In this context it is noteworthy that out of the 50 years of its existence, the Chinese space programme was under the direct control of the PLA for more than three decades. It was only in the reforms era that the Chinese made an attempt to 'civilianise' the space programme by transferring control from the PLA to the Commission of Science Technology and Industry for National Defence (COSTIND). Nevertheless the fact of the matter is that COSTIND retained close links with the PLA since in addition to the space programme, it was also responsible for R&D and production of military hardware of all varieties. If a rough Indian analogy could be drawn, it would as if in addition to its other duties, the DRDO was also given the charge of ISRO! In stark contrast to the Chinese system, the more than six degrees of separation between the Indian space programme and the military establishment are well known. Thankfully recent years have seen a greater synchrony between India space capabilities and her defence needs.

Chinese Space Industry

Analogous to NASA and our own ISRO, China National Space Agency (CNSA) is the apex policy making body of the Chinese space programme. It is also responsible for international cooperation and presents the 'civilian' face of the Chinese space industry to the rest of the world. However interestingly, it is an internal structure of the Commission of Science Technology and Industry for National Defence (COSTIND) [which has been recently reorganized as the State Administration of Science Technology and Industry for National Defence (SASTIND)]. The two major Chinese corporations which actually design produce and launch the Chinese space assets are China Aerospace Science and Technology Corporation (CASC) and China Aerospace Science and Industry Corporation (CASIC). Both are gigantic organizations with approximately 100,000 employees each. Both work on the unique Chinese model public sector companies run on the lines of private corporations. Insofar as the space programme is concerned, CASC is the more prominent of the two and said to be actually 'running' the space programme. It produces the Shenzhou series of spacecraft, the Long March series of launch vehicles, and almost all satellites. In addition, CASC is also a major producer of missiles and other military hardware. The production of CASIC on the other hand, is skewed more in favour of military than space hardware. Its products include spacecraft, telecommunication equipment, missiles, specialist vehicles, machinery etc.

ISRO on the other hand, has less than 15,000 employees, is primarily engaged in producing satellites and launch vehicles, and is definitely not a part of the Indian military industry. While it may be true that the large size of the Chinese corporations may not be a true indicator of the actual size of the Chinese space industry as they are engaged in other activities also, it cannot be denied that the Chinese policy makers retain the option to divert resources to the space programme at short notice. Thus overall China has a massive lead over India in the size and capability of its space industry.

Size and Ambition of Space Programmes

Both India and China have ambitious space programmes with China enjoying a definitive edge over India. While China has already achieved human spaceflight, India has still some way to go before it can boast of this feat. China also boasts of a much more evolved launch vehicle capability based on the Long March series which has run into six families of launch vehicles till now. The maximum capability for GTO of the Long March family is reported to be approximately 14 tons. China is also in the process of developing the a new series of solid fuel launch vehicles named the KT series which will give it the much sought 'launch-on-demand' capability. India on the other hand has two main variants in its launch vehicle family viz the PSLV series and the GSLV series. While the versatile PSLV series has emerged as the work-horse of the space programme India hopes to achieve GTO capability of 5 tons with the still under development GSLV Mk III.

In addition to launch vehicles, China has a large number of satellites encompassing a wide variety of roles. It has the DFH series satellites for telecommunications, the FY series for meteorology, the FSW series recoverable satellites and the ZY series remote-sensing satellites. In addition are the SJ series scientific and experimental satellites, the Beidou series navigation and positioning satellites, the HY series ocean satellites and a number of microsatellites (some with foreign collaboration). India on the other hand has a relatively smaller family of satellites with the INSAT series and the IRS series forming the backbone of the Indian satellite programme. India too has a variety of special purpose satellites like Oceansat, RISAT-2, scientific research satellites and micro-satellites. By all accounts the Indian communication satellite capability is a shade better than the Chinese. India also scores over China in the field of remote-sensing satellites. In fact the *Space Competitiveness Index 2009* developed by the Futron Corporation of the US has called India the 'global leader in remote-sensing'.

While the future plans of both nations include lunar exploration and Mars exploration missions in the near future, China has an immense lead over India both in the ambition and the extent of its space programme. This is evident from the statement of Luo Ge of the China National Space Agency (CNSA) made in an international symposium in 2006- "Generally speaking, in the coming 5-8 years, we will be launching about 100 satellites". He also announced plans for a lunar rover, an orbiting Spacelab and a possible lunar landing prompting one of the delegates to respond- "Man oh man ... they're not kidding around." It is evident that what to talk of India, even developed countries will be hard pressed to match such capability.

Space Budgets

China also enjoys a substantial edge over India in the size of the space budget. Conservative estimates indicate that the Chinese space budget is in the region of US $ 1.3 billion plus. In comparison the declared Indian space budget is US $ 892 million. If the Chinese tendency of keeping their actual budget under wraps is taken into account, it would be safe to assume that it would slightly less than double the Indian space budget. This difference in size and budgets becomes evident when one compares the variety of space 'products' of the two space industries. Therefore it may be safely concluded that overall the balance of power is tilted in China's favour.

Chinese Space Warfare Capabilities

Space and National Security

It would be highly erroneous to think that the Chinese space programme is only India-specific or regional in ambition. China surely has more ambitious plans than just dominating Asia. Nevertheless, India being the immediate neighbour and perhaps a competing power-centre, cannot afford to ignore the security implications of the untrammelled rise of Chinese military space capabilities. The official Chinese view of integrating space assets into the national security calculus is enunciated quite clearly in the White Paper issued by the Chinese government entitled -"China's Space Activities" 2006. It states the aims of the Chinese space programme as:-

- ♦ To **explore** outer space, and learn more about the cosmos and the Earth.

- ♦ To utilize outer space **for peaceful purposes**, promote mankind's civilization and social progress, and benefit the whole of mankind.

- ♦ To meet the growing demands of economic construction, **national security**, science and technology development and social progress, protect China's national interests and build up the **comprehensive national strength**.

The White paper further goes on to state - "Priority is given to upgrading technologies and products in the nuclear, space, aviation, shipbuilding, weaponry, electronics and other defence-related industries, so as to form a cluster of high-tech industries to drive the growth of China's economy...... Major scientific and technological projects, such as manned space flights and the Lunar Probe Project, are being carried out to spur the leapfrogging development of high-tech enterprises combining military and civilian needs and to bring about overall improvements in defence-related science and technology..... As a result, a fairly mature scientific and technological infrastructure is taking shape, which is well-configured, multi-functional, efficient and based on close cooperation between the military and civilian sectors."

It thus becomes obvious that while like most other nations, China too does not advocate militarisation of space; the Chinese do not seem to be averse to leveraging their space capability for national security and power projection. China is a part of international committees like UN COPUOS (*United Nations* Committee on the Peaceful Uses of Outer Space) and has recently moved a resolution seeking a ban on offensive activities in space in conjunction with Russia. Nevertheless what is important from the Indian perspective is the policy emphasis both on civil and military uses of space projects. This is best exemplified in the words of President Hu Jintao in 2006- "*We need to build an innovative system of defence science and technology..... that* **integrates military and civilian scientific-technological resources**, *and that organically integrates basic research, applied R&D, product designing and manufacturing, and procurement of technologies and products to create a good structure under which* **military and civilian technologies are shared and mutually transferable**"

Military Capabilities in Space

Nowhere is the definitive edge enjoyed by China over India in space more accentuated than in the field of military satellites. Ever since the launch of its space programme, China has always had a few satellites dedicated for military communications and remote-sensing. China is also known to have developed ELINT/SIGINT satellites in the past with varied degrees of success. This has included the JSSW series (discontinued in the 1970's) and some SJ series scientific satellites. The Chinese are also known to have tried to enhance their SIGINT capabilities by making an abortive bid to acquire two satellites in the open market from Hughes Space & Communications in 1996. Thus Chinese interest in space based ELINT/SIGINT assets is well established. As per some reports, even some of the Shenzhou manned spacecraft have carried payloads consistent with SIGINT missions.

Insofar as military communications are concerned, PLA launched a dedicated military communication satellite, FH-1 in 2000, the first of five satellites planned for the Qu Dian C4I system, modelled on the US JTIDS. When fully deployed, the Qu Dian system with a dedicated satellite constellation will provide real-time tactical communications and data transfer capabilities to PLA commanders to conduct effective joint operations. Another military communication satellite, the ShenTong-1 (ST-1) was launched in November 2003. In addition to communication satellites, China has also launched the Tianlian data relay satellite to support its manned spaceflight programme considerably enhancing the Chinese reach.

Recent developments have seen a substantial improvement in Chinese remote-sensing capabilities with a gradual migration from film recovery systems to real-time digital data downlinks. China has also embarked on an ambitious Positioning Navigation and Timing (PNT) programme based on Beidou satellites which is being touted as a regional competitor to the American GPS. Thus it is increasingly becoming clear that Chinese space based C3I capabilities are increasing at such a rapid pace that it may become difficult for India to offset the Chinese edge unless urgent steps are taken to increase Indian military presence in space.

But more than mere military satellites, it is the growing Chinese offensive capability in space which should be worrying Indian policy makers. China has been carrying out R&D on fundamental technologies applicable to ASAT weapons system since the 1960s. The Central committee of Communist party has reportedly given the highest priority to development of anti-surveillance ASAT systems. The Chinese have concentrated their ASAT efforts in developing ground-based high energy lasers (HEL), ground or air launched interceptor missiles, high power microwaves, parasitic satellites, micro-satellites and 'hunter-killer' satellites. In addition to the famous ASAT test of 2007, in August 2006, China had fired high-power lasers at American intelligence satellites flying over its territory and caused disruption. Another DoD reports suggest that China may also be developing systems to jam US navigation satellite signals. In the words of Lt Gen Kevin Campbell, commander of the U.S. Army Space and Missile Defense Command – "(China will be capable) of taking out a number of communications capabilities over a theater of war". This emphasis on ASAT systems is suggestive that China's may be keen to develop have a long term capability to fight future space wars, if the need so arises.

In the context of the Chinese offensive space warfare capabilities the events which led to the Shenzhou 7 controversy in 2008 are also noteworthy. The spacecraft passed unusually close (45 km) to the International Space Station (ISS). There was little margin for error. At that time the $100 billion space station had two Russians and one American aboard. Four hours before Shenzhou's point of closest approach to the space station, it launched 40 kg manoeuvrable microsatellite BX-1 which contained two cameras and communication gear. Many analysts speculated that keeping in mind China's track record of using all Shenzhou missions since 1999 for dual military-civil role, this manoeuvre might have been part of a test of a new ASAT technology.

Chinese Space Doctrines

From the aims and objectives of the Chinese space programme it is abundantly clear that the China considers its space capabilities as an irrefutable part of her national defence matrix and an essential part of battle planning. In formulating its own space doctrines, Chinese military theorists have studied US and Soviet/Russian space doctrines on space war in detail in order to evolve their own thinking. Broadly in alignment with the western theories, Chinese space warfare doctrines too fall in two broad categories:-

- **High Ground Doctrine.** This includes what the Chinese military analysts call 'Battlefield Combatting' which is akin in concept and execution as the 'Space control' theory. This doctrine entails development of offensive ASAT or SBSW (Space based strike weapons) and aims to control a part of outer space to use it for enhancing own operations and denying its use to the enemy. This theory is similar to Aerospace control and Sea control theories of terrestrial operations and seeks to control outer space in a similar fashion. In concept and execution Chinese theories seem to be influenced by the 'High Ground' or the 'High Frontier' doctrine of the Americans. In the words of one of the leading Chinese space theorists, Maj Gen Liu Jixian of the Chinese Academy of Military Sciences- "*Whoever controls space controls initiative in war*". This statement succinctly sums up the Chinese attitude to space warfare.

- **Force Enhancement Doctrine.** This doctrine is more 'peaceful' or 'defensive' in nature and is geared towards exploiting space assets to support the conduct and execution of terrestrial operations. The Chinese call it 'Information supporting' and include activities like Intelligence, navigation, positioning, communications etc in its ambit. This is perhaps the most common use of space assets for military purposes and by and large within the ambit of international space law. While China has a substantial number of space assets deployed in this role, it seems to be set on a trajectory to graduate from mere force enhancement to space domination and control.

Although China is developing and has developed capabilities to support both doctrines, the Chinese long-term interest in ASAT weapons and micro-satellites is perhaps indicative that 'High Ground' space doctrine is acquiring prominence in Chinese strategic thought. China's military theorists also view ASAT and offensive space capabilities as means to offset the asymmetric advantage enjoyed by the US. China is also uneasy about US BMD developments and some Chinese writings state that "*The US is trying to build a strategic external border in space*". In the words of one of the leading Chinese military space theorists Maj Gen Cai Fengzhen- "*Control of portions of outer space is a natural extension of other forms of territorial control*" and "*space control today is the way to guarantee the control of airspace...... and is an absolute necessity for conducting modern informationalised warfare*". Other analysts like Senior Col Zhang Zhiwei of Nanjing Army Command Academy argue that *Space supremacy must be an integral part of other forms of supremacy over the battlefield.* Some theorists advocate- space be used to "*carry out war between space platforms and to attack strategic surface and air targets*".

The Chinese thoughts on 'sovereignty' over space are also interesting. While China is a signatory to most international conventions and protocols on space and subscribes to the theory that space is the 'common heritage' of mankind, there are rumblings in the military establishment that could point to a possible change in the future. It is well known that China has been sensitive to military reconnaissance of its landmass and EEZ by satellites and some Chinese analysts have compared reconnaissance to 'battlefield preparation'. These fears were further accentuated by the incident when satellite pictures of China's new Jin class submarine which appeared on Google Earth on 5 Jul 07. This incident caused much consternation and breast beating in the PLA. As a result some Chinese military theorists have started to argue that concept of national sovereignty be extended to outer space as well, although this is not the official position of the Chinese establishment.

Conclusion

In conclusion it is obvious that PLA sees war in space as an integral part of military operations and advocates use of both offensive and defensive operations in outer space. Space is thus a key component of the Chinese

RMA and a crucial component of its national security strategy. Not only does China has a substantial space capability to support surface operations by way of navigation, targeting, ISR etc, but it is one of the few nations to have carried out a successful ASAT test in 2007. Interestingly, post the ASAT test, China proposed a draft treaty on 'Prevention of the Placement of Weapons in Outer Space and the Threat of Use of Force Against Outer Space Objects' jointly with Russia. While some analysts see this as a change of heart prompted by the international outcry over the space debris created by the test which endangered many space objects. Others see it a form of 'Legal Warfare' consistent with the Chinese record of utilising international law to prevent its potential future competitors from acquiring similar capabilities. What are the real Chinese motives behind this rather surprising move remains a moot question.

Session III : Discussion

Issues Raised

Do we know anything about PLA's training patterns and philosophy? What are the PLA Navy and Air Force aiming for?

Response

Generally, training patterns and philosophy behind People's Liberation Army, Navy and Air Force would give some idea of what the Chinese Armed Forces themselves must be thinking about. They say the same thing, *'Many countries do train, as you will fight'*. Training gives an indication and is guided by the operational planning department of a country. The Chinese have published a book which mentions '24 Operational Plans' and gives instructions as to how the China's Army, Navy, Air Forces and Rocket Forces would be involved in counter attack campaigns to meet various contingencies. Some of these 24 Operational Plans are related to:-

(a) Mountain Warfare.

(b) Cover for submarines to penetrate an island blockade of China.

(c) How to eliminate enemy airfields in a surprise attack?

(d) Joint missions by missile forces, air force, infantry including air borne forces in a surprise attack.

(e) How Chinese forces can conduct joint operations against landing forces?

For example, 'Joint Nuclear Counter Attack Campaign' indicates that the Chinese approach seems to be, "to wait, not to have nuclear retaliation within an hour or 15 minutes; but to wait for a period of days or upto a week" and this particular training campaign has to do with Second Artillery Forces. It also mentions how the PLA Navy and Air Force are involved in counter attack campaigns.

The importance of this book can be realised fully only if its English translation is made. The fact that its Chief Editor is the former Director of Operations for the entire Chinese Armed Forces, it does give some idea about the Chinese training philosophy. Their focus on counter attacks suggests that, 'China lives in a world of threats' – one of the scenarios is 'Counter Landing Campaigns'. China has identified a number of beaches that are perceived to be vulnerable; and needs to maintain forces against amphibious landings by unnamed foreign countries.

In terms of money, China has earmarked $ 500 billion each for the PLA Navy and the Air Force – and more than that for the ground forces. For them to acquire weapons to meet these training scenarios would be very expensive. Actually, the American and Indian soft power should assure China that no foreign country has any aggressive attack plans against them. On the other hand, their *'training scenarios'* frighten the rest of the world; and that if China decides to follow the spirit of Confucius, they could devote all their money for solving numerous internal problems – which everyone is aware of.

Issue Raised

The Chinese nuclear strategy has been presented today in a very supplicative way, arguing that the USA and Russia should take the lead in creating a nuclear weapon free world. China has also advocated and strenuously asked all the countries long ago to join NPT. What kind of measures China itself can take in order to convince the entire world that they are very serious about a nuclear weapon free world?

Response

China has taken some measures to indicate that they take the concept of nuclear weapon free world seriously. The first one is about the CTBT and the second one is on fissile materials cut off treaty. The Chinese have also shown their urgency by playing a constructive role in next year's NPT Review Conference. Actually, all these measures have not yet resulted into concrete steps because majority of the Chinese nuclear arms controllers think that the USA should ratify the CTBT first and China will follow suit. However, some Chinese analysts do think that they ought to take the lead to ratify the CTBT as that would make it easier for Obama to persuade the US Senate to ratify the treaty. In the process of debate, China has already dropped some pre-conditions to put the treaty negotiations in Geneva at the Conference on Disarmament (CD) on the table. China may not have gone far enough as yet, but, may be would do so now, especially at the next years NPT Review Conference.

Issue Raised

Is there any possibility for China to replace the USA to be the number one military budget country in the world in the next 10 to 20 years?

Responses

(a) The answer is 'yes'. China can replace the USA as number one defence spender in the world in the next 20 years. This is possible. Comparing defence budgets of other countries is always an ongoing exercise. According to Rand Corporation studies, China's defence spending is relatively low – 3 per cent of its GDP, whereas the USA and Russia's defence spending exceeded 30 per cent of their GDP. The Chinese are right when their soft power projection says that, their defence spending - 1.5 to 3 per cent of GDP is quite low in comparison with other countries. It is so, because it is intended to persuade other countries to remain complacent, not to engage in military planning or weapons acquisition and also not take the rise of China's military power as a serious matter. This is the goal of soft power. As one speaker said yesterday, 'China is always right'. This is part of soft power.

(b) But there is another important side to the case. It takes at least 10 years to prepare forces to meet the security challenges through operational goals and plans. The training has to include 'low' and 'worst' case scenarios. Although the chances of China hurting India, as of now, seem to be low, but the possibility of something like 1962 happening again has to be taken into consideration by the strategic thinkers and planners. They perforce have to keep track of overall Chinese military modernisation and to maintain pressure on DRDO to develop weapon systems indigenously.

(c) Every country has a right to plan and prepare its forces to defend its territory. So, the military modernisation of China should not be branded as a threat.

(d) Neighbouring and big countries are apprehensive about the Chinese military modernisation and have got a problem in assuaging the feeling of insecurity emanating from this phenomenon. Therefore, it should continue to be assessed and discussed.

Session III: Chairman's Concluding Remarks

It was my great pleasure to have chaired this session. The five panellists have given us a great deal of knowledge from which the strategic community can learn much. I am sure this discussion will help the strategic discourse. We need more of these sessions to keep abreast with developments in the neighbourhood and the world.

REGIONAL IMPLICATIONS OF CHINA'S RISE : BUILDING AN ENDURING POWER EQUATION IN ASIA

FOURTH SESSION

Chairman	Shri K Raghunath, IFS (Retd)
First Paper	Professor Han Hua , SIS Peking University
Second Paper	Vice Admiral Hideaki Kaneda (Retd) , Okazaki Institute, Japan
Third Paper	Professor Jaeho Hwang, Korean Institute for Defence Analyses
Fourth Paper	Professor Sujit Dutta, Jamia Milia University
Discussion	
Closing Remarks	Shri Shiv Shankar Menon, IFS Foreign Secretary

Session IV : Chairman's Opening Remarks

Ambassador K Raghunath

First of all, I join the USI in welcoming all the members of the esteemed audience and the distinguished panellists. I would also like to join you in thanking USI for organising this very wide ranging and exhaustive seminar. I would like to underline the fact that they are redoubtable experts in their own respective fields and have also been very articulate and active in educating the public in their own countries and also in communication with the outside world – the strategic community in other countries including India. I must also add, with respect to our participants from China, Japan and Korea that we value their involvement in Track-II communication with us. We value the contribution they have made in promoting cooperation, understanding and goodwill both bilaterally and in the multilateral context. Our participant from India, Professor Sujit Dutta is well known as a prominent member of the strategic community here in India. His presence here underlines the fact that he represents the growing interest in 'China Studies' in India. The point that our participants from abroad need to take note of is that China is a serious subject in India.

I begin with a few preparatory remarks to reiterate some truisms which have been visited earlier, because it would be useful to do so. First of all of course, the terminology – the word 'rise' which has been used very frequently here. I do not wish to pre-empt our Chinese friends but I do recognise from the literature on the subject and especially from what has been said in various fora by spokesmen from China that they would like to rectify this term in the old Confucian sense. I would leave this task to our

friends from China but I would like to point out here that this term is actually
a reflection of 'perceptions' only and it does not carry any particularly loaded
connotation. It's a shorthand code-word, so you may interpret that word in
any other way.

The subject of this particular session is: 'Regional Implications of
China's Rise and Building an Enduring Power Equation in Asia'. This
particular rubric in some fashion has been replicated in seminars held in
this city a few days ago and some of the worthies who organised these
seminars are either present or were present in this hall yesterday. For
example, ICWA seminar talked about *Prospects for Partnership'.* These
are variations and two sides of the same coin. I underline this point because
in this particular seminar there is a focus on one specific aspect, which is
covered in the term *'Power Equations'.* That is important because this
terminology was also chosen deliberately and meant to convey some
meanings. I hardly need add that both these aspects are conveyed or
represented in the two different seminars – today's and the one I referred
to. They are actually complementary. This is a truism, but in the context of
regional power equations and regional cooperation it needs to be said that
any relationship whether bilateral or multilateral, particularly in the regional
context, has two dimensions. One is a very strong and inherent element of
cooperation, partnership; harmony, dependence of course,
interdependence if you like, and at the same time also an element of
potential conflict; and the other is disharmony, confrontation, tension, conflict
etc. In order to build a stable and dynamic kind of power equation you
need really to make sure that the first of these two dimensions is maximised
and the second is minimised. I am putting it very simply but this is a very
difficult task, especially given the proximity and the neighbourhood factor
in a regional onslaught. So, statesmanship really means cultivating all the
possibilities and potential for cooperation and for partnership and at the
same time taking a realistic view of the other aspect i.e. idealism without
illusions. I think that is a good formula because we are really talking about
an approach to building power equations, in this region, which is devoid of

both extremes of *utopianism*, and also devoid of obsessive real politic. This is doable and in fact that is really the task ahead for all those who are involved in advancing or promoting regional cooperation. With good faith and vision these things can be done. Seminars like this itself underlines the point. It is significant that there is a growing preoccupation with bringing about an architecture of regional security and cooperation in our part of the world. Just as well, because unless we do this, we are losing something in terms of realising the national potential. This is a thought that I would like to leave with you.

There is one more aspect which needs attention. This refers to the title of this session – 'Enduring Power Equation'. If you compare it with the aspect of 'cooperation'; i.e. economic cooperation and other types of functional cooperation, in substantive areas, it certainly helps to moderate the climate and creates a milieu for cooperation. But this is not a sufficient condition. It is unfortunately the case that we need to address the *'security'* aspect independently of anything else and it has to be done. Once we face that reality then we are on good ground and that is why this particular seminar is important.

Before I conclude, I want to flag a few points about; *What needs to be done?* These general principles would also draw attention to something that the panellists would be addressing. We need to understand : Why things are not necessarily shaping the way they should at a given point of time? This is the question that has to be answered. On the positive side, the basic requirements are:

(a) Understanding and respecting the legitimate national aspirations and national   interests of every big and small country and also the specific circumstances of each country would enable us to understand why certain decisions are taken. We presume that they are taken in good faith most of the time, and taking into account the neighbourhood location, history and other such factors.

(b) Equal legitimate security at a minimal possible cost.

(c) 'Power Equation', yes. But we have to eschew some of the crimes and follies of the 19th Century which led to terrible catastrophes. Asia, is not condemned to repeat all the mistakes of Europe, provided we are aware that some of the old constructs like 'balance of power', 'spheres of influence', 'the great game', the idea of a 'dominant power', are all outmoded. There has to be a conscious effort to factor them out and do something else.

(d) The fact is that all of us face common challenges – regional challenges, global challenges which bind us together. Terrorism is one of them. I would underline here that anyone who believes that terrorism in one part of the world or in one part of a region is the problem peculiar to that part of the region is asking for trouble. A heavy price would have to be paid for that kind of approach. *Secondly*, there are other security related aspects not excluding disarmament (including nuclear disarmament), the economic aspect, ecology and other problems like natural disasters, culture, human welfare and so on.

(e) It is a well known principle, that security is not related to the military dimension alone – comprehensive national strength, comprehensive national security, all very valid concepts, but the *'military-political'* aspect is important. That is what is going to be focused on here.

(f) The WHO definition of health, applies to security and to power equations and to cooperation. But health is not merely freedom from illness and disease; it is a positive state of being and that is what one looks for.

Dynamic and stable equilibria and relations in which problems are discussed consensually are important. There would be some specific questions which would be addressed by the panelists e.g. who are the powers we are talking about? There are some countries which are not clearly defined as being Asian. The USA of course is a case in point. There are others in Oceania, Australia and New Zealand, Russia, where do they fit in. I think this is a matter of definition because the term Asia itself has to be looked at carefully. So, this question I hope will be addressed when we talk about power equations.

Then the role of Track-II dialogue is extremely important. All the points that I have mentioned have been examined and discussed threadbare during this particular seminar yesterday. However, new insights are always welcome and they are needed. This search for truth helps us to move from one state to the other. I am sure this seminar, through the wisdom, expertise and experience of our panellists would add to the stock of awareness or the storehouse of solutions that we might have. In that spirit, I would like to invite the panelists to proceed with their presentations.

Session IV : First Paper

Professor Han Hua

{This presentation is limited to the speaker's observations based on discussion in earlier sessions}

Presently, China is facing a 'security dilemma'. China feels sandwiched between a established power like the USA and its neighbours on the other side. How to reassure both sides, about its thinking and security intentions, is a very challenging job. Sometimes, it feels that the USA is a strategic challenge and most pressures come from the US side. It has to prepare for these challenges but at the same time there is a feeling that if Chinese do something to upgrade their capabilities, other countries around it or other areas feel threatened. How should it balance against these threats in two directions? The thinkers have faith in the Chinese wisdom, but they would need to learn more about diplomacy to resolve this dilemma.

The second point about the rise of China is that dealing with a rising power is not a one way solution. Although China should do something to decrease threat perceptions and sensitivities of other countries, but at the same time, the established powers and neighbours should also review their approach towards the rising power. How they would do that would be meaningful for China. China's policy is made by their overall evaluation of the international environment. China needs a peaceful environment for sustaining its economic development. The Chinese say, *"you can choose the way you live but you cannot choose where you are staying or located"*. China has the most number of neighbouring states around it. That is why China's rise has implications for other regions, – which may not be limited only to East Asia and South Asia or South East Asia. It is indeed very challenging for China to take into consideration the sensitivities and perspectives of so many neighbouring countries.

The third point is about China's strategic capabilities and overall military capability build up. How the military thinks about its role and probable postures? In China, or may be in other countries like India too, the military people tend to talk more about, worst case scenarios. They have to prepare for the worst scenario but at the same time there is another Chinese saying, *"you have to prepare for the worst but at the same time you have to pursue the most favourable outcome"*.

Military is only part of the overall policy making community in China and China is not a militarily controlled country. You should note that in China's nine member Standing Committee, Hu Jintao is the only one chief military commander – the rest are non military officers. Therefore, they have civilian culture. They do have civilian control over the military. We do not think Chinese military dominates decision making – that is for sure. The policies are made by the leadership or working groups and not by the military. But, at the same time, China is a responsible power. Perhaps, this is not what you would like to hear. China tries its best to reassure its neighbours and other countries that its rise would be peaceful in the 21st Century.

Session IV: Second Paper

Mr Hideaki Kaneda

This paper covers military and naval matters related to multilateral cooperation for Sea Lanes of Communication (SLOC) security. The observations on *'Rising Importance of Sea Lanes'* will cover the following aspects:-

(a) Confrontation in Korean peninsula and across Taiwan straits.

(b) Rapid build-up of the Chinese Military Power.

(c) Disputes over territories in South China Sea, East China Sea and other places.

(d) Maritime interests in the vicinity of Japan – dispute with China in East China Sea.

(e) Proliferation of WMD and Ballistic Missiles.

(f) International Terrorism and Piracy, specially in Malacca and Singapore Straits.

(g) Organised illegal activities at sea and the 'Strategic Chinese bases in the Vital Sea Lanes'; i.e. 'String of Pearls'.

"Security of sea Lanes" is a common key word in discussing all these issues. Japan, the USA as well as regional countries should note that 'multilateral cooperation' would be 'vital for SLOC'. Not only security but regional economy and stability also depend on security of SLOC. Security of SLOC should be considered based on the concept of 'Broad Sea Lanes' protection. A sea lane does not end in a 'Single Region'. Broad Sea Lanes

(BSL) running through the Indian Ocean, via Asia-Pacific to the Oceania or South Pacific in expanded Asia, becomes vital as 'lifelines' to meet security and economic needs of the 'Unified Region'. Therefore, there are emerging needs for multilateral cooperation between reliable and like-minded maritime powers to ensure the security of BSL in expanded Asia. The core maritime power would be centred around Japan as well as the USA in the North and East; and in the East-West-South Expanded Asia, India, Japan, the USA and Australia would be important players.

Now let us take a look at the historical relationships amongst the related countries. First is the long Japan-US maritime alliance, which is viewed as a 'core' military alliance. The deepening and widening of the Japan-US alliance was assured and confirmed at the recent visit of Mr Obama to Japan. Obama and Hatoyama have assured of a 'tight and equal relationship' in their core role for security of BSL because of high expectations from Japan and the USA.

Maritime security partnership between Japan-India-US (JIUS) is a key to the relationships. The Indian Ocean has strategic importance across the world. Earlier the USA referred to it as *'an arc of instability'*, it should now be changed to read as *'an arc of inseparability'*. Each of these countries recognises the need for cooperation on security of SLOC in East-West expanded Asia. So far there is no formal 'trilateral' security arrangement between them. From the Japanese perspective a global partnership has been formed through the India-US relationship since the meeting between President Bush and Prime Minister Manmohan Singh in 2005. Defence cooperation guidelines in the same year set a new framework for India-US defence relationship which included the maritime domain also. The US Department of Defence (DoD) announced enhancement of security cooperation with India which included maritime security in 2006. It was followed by meeting between Mr Manmohan Singh and Mr Gates in 2008; and also Mr Singh's meeting with Mr Obama in Nov 2009. There has been a substantial increase in cooperation through maritime exercises such as 'Malabar' in 2007.

The main feature of Japan-India relationship is a partnership of historical sympathy. It is based on common values of freedom and democracy. Substantial joint agreements / statements have been published to give new dimension to the road map of strategic global partnership. Recently, these have been followed up by two joint statements on security cooperation by Japanese Prime Ministers Abe, Fukuda and Aso with Prime Minister Manmohan Singh in 2006, 2007 and 2008. During Nov 2009, Japanese Minister of Defence Katazawa and Indian Defence Minister Anthony have also met. Japanese Prime Minister Hatoyama's visit to India is also planned towards the end of 2009. In 2009 the Indian destroyer which participated in the Chinese International Review, on it's way back after that, had a good exercise with Japan to which the USA was also invited.

In the North-West expanded Asia, Japan, Australia, US (JAUS) have a maritime alliance. They had the first trilateral summit in Syndey in 2007. Japan and the USA urged security cooperation with Australia and India at the '2+2' Ministerial Meeting in 2007. Former Prime Minister Fukuda pushed his Trilateral Strategic Dialogue and the Australian Prime Minister Rudd confirmed the unchanged positive attitude towards it. Even though Japan, the USA and Australia do not have any treaty arrangements but they do have Trilateral Semi-Alliance and several cooperative security activities. Many cooperative exercises were held in 2007 and 2008, which included the P3-C's Exercises in 2007.

Amongst bilateral relationships, the US-Australia alliance is akin to blood relationship. Australian-United States Ministerial Consultations (AUSMIN) and Australian, New Zealand and United States Security Treaty (ANZUS) are maritime alliances which strengthen the fabric of peace in the Asia Pacific. The new US administration has confirmed bilateral policy, on issues such as Iraq, BMD, anti-terrorism etc. They have historical ties for cooperation on regional and global security issues to facilitate inter-operability which includes missile defence. There is also increasing defence cooperation in Iraq and international Disaster Relief Operations (DRO).

Japan-Australia is not an alliance but a semi-alliance. They share a strong maritime partnership based on democratic values. There was a joint declaration on security cooperation between Abe and Mr Howard in 2007. Since then Ministerial Security Meetings have continued. In 2008, a Memorandum on Japan-Australia Defence Cooperation was signed. Both countries have substantial cooperation and conduct frequent joint exercises since 1996.

Next is the Japanese perspective on India-Australia relations. Australia is reshaping its policy toward India, from Howard to Rudd, on security around China. Is it possible to get a strong breakthrough on development of defence cooperation? Refer to Australian Minister for Foreign Affairs Stephen Smith's statement in February 2008. Quadrilateral Maritime Cooperation is difficult instantly. However, JIUS and JAUS trilateral cooperation would be possible in the future.

JIUS Maritime Security partnership and JAUS Maritime Semi-alliance should take responsibilities appropriate to their national power as major stakeholders of maritime security coalition with other democratic maritime powers for security of Broad Sea Lanes – JIUS in East West and JAUS in North South expanded Asia.

What is Maritime Security Coalition? It must be a nation to nation coalition with a common objective – to maintain and secure safe and free use of 'ocean's sea lanes' from the peacetime to emergency situations. Network of activities based on 'common values' – common value must be a key word in such interactions, not a treaty, but maritime coalition based on strong mutual trust, responsibility of each nation proportionate to its national situation and capacity.

What should be the pre-condition for Maritime Security Coalition? It should be possible to share three basic interests in the maritime domain with others. First is *'existence'* i.e. security interests, second would be *'prosperity'* i.e. economic interests; and third one is *'identity'*. Common values that would interest all are: disaster relief, restoration, rescue and conservation of environment/resources in maritime domain. It would be expected of the member countries that their actions are guided by democratic norms and based on the concept of public good and service to others. Likeminded democratic countries would not have disputes over maritime sovereignty or interests and would adhere to international norms in resolving problems in a fair manner. Each member of JIUS or JAUS would stand for maritime security of the four coalition countries and would be eager to do so in a positive manner. Japan's active interest in improving international security is addressed in the National Defence Programme Guidelines (NDPG) which is like QDR in the USA. India's policy of *'more cooperation with others in maritime domain'* was stated by Admiral Sureesh Mehta. The USA's willingness for *'more cooperation with others'* in Global Maritime Partnership was confirmed by Admiral Roughead. Australia's *'Stronger Security Partnership with others'* is stated in Defence White Paper 2009.

The main subject is 'Broad Maritime Security Coalition (BMSC)'. JIUS Maritime Security Coalition in East-West expanded Asia should be tied up with JAUS Maritime Security Coordination in North-South expanded Asia, towards constituting BMSC in the whole expanded Asia in the future. May be, that would include the South Pacific island nations or such countries also. Broad Maritime Security Coalition should eventually develop towards global stage – Japan's BMSC Initiative coincides with Japan's Diplomatic Policy. Former Prime Minister Abe said 'the coalition of nations is based on common values. Former Prime Minister Fukuda said, 'synergy' with Japan-US Alliance and *'diplomacy'* towards Asia. Former Prime Minister Aso talked of 'Arc of freedom and prosperity'. The current prime minister

Hatoyama said, *'Fraternity, diplomacy and East Asia community'*. These are very important things for us, if we have to make the coalition succeed.

We need deep cooperation with ASEAN countries because it is the geographic centre of expanded Asia. Many strategic or regional policy frameworks, are needed. Strait of Malacca is vital as a choke point. Illegal activity in the vast waters including island areas needs to be checked. Some of them are reliable democratic maritime powers whereas others have relatively weaker navy and coast guards. Capacity building and humanitarian support by Japan and other countries is essential.

We need to constitute the JIUS and JAUS Maritime Security Coalition with democratic power groups in East-West and North-South expanded Asia. Aiming for unification of 2+2 or specific security channels might be suitable. Coordinating soft maritime cooperation by every coastal state including China is important in addition to existing regional cooperative agreements: Asian Regional Forum (ARF), Western Pacific Naval Symposium (WPNS), Indian Ocean Naval Symposium (IONS), or Japan's new initiative in East West community support.

Chairman's Remarks

Thank you Admiral Kaneda for your very comprehensive and in depth treatment of a very specific and important aspect of the security structures and security arrangements in our region. There is much food for thought here, not only for Admirals but for all of us who are engaged with this idea of promoting stable structures of cooperation and security in this region.

Session IV : Third Paper

Professor Jaeho Hwang

The hot topic during President Obama's recent visit to Asia was *'China's Rise'*. It is evident from frequent references to the expression 'the G2 era' that we are now witnessing the coming of US-China 'Bipolar era'. This also signifies the sharing of mutual concerns amongst countries around the world - *How to respond to this China, that is shoulder to shoulder with the USA?* South Korea is no exception. May be, some states may not agree with this logic. Even China itself denies the use of expression G2. However for China's neighbours, such as South Korea, the 'Rise of China' is not a matter of 'if' but a reality of 'when' that happens!

Climate change is becoming a hot agenda for international community and the issue has already unravelled in South Korea's security environment. We are now thinking about questions of what sort of air we breathe and in what kind of climate we must live in. The rise of China has come to dominate South Korean way of thinking. The topic of my presentation today is, *'South Korea's perspective on China's rise'*. There are basically three questions. First, how has the world framework changed? Second, can China become the world's number one superpower? Third, what are the strategy implications for South Korea's security, given China's rise? The first is, *'Need for long term changes to the framework'*, the second, *'Prospects and the immediate short term changes'*, and finally, *'An explanation of South Korea's policy towards China'*.

Perhaps, not looking as far ahead as the year 2050; but, just 15 years from now, by 2025 the international order is expected to change into a multi-polar power shift, with the USA and China as core countries. We can predict the possibility of China becoming a super power in a future time frame but not by the year 2025. Theoretically, a country aspiring to become a superpower must meet three criteria – capability, will and recognition. By 2025, China would probably fail to meet all three. However, it would attain the state of quasi-superpower by 2025. To reach that state China would have to overcome several political, economic and security obstacles.

Together with long term predictions, we need to examine short term changes in the framework. First, the USA is reconfiguring policy on better lines now. Bush's diplomacy weakened cooperation between major powers, allies and friendly nations. The Obama Administration is strengthening cooperation with powers and allies and even extending hand to hostile countries. The international community is welcoming and embracing President Obama. This is a new chance for the US initiative. Hu Jintao's diplomatic strategy is 'harmonious world'. Harmony is regarded as the universal value of global order and is dependent on soft power. However, China's 'harmonious world' benefited relatively speaking from the US indifference and lack of interest in the region during the Bush period and it has been successful so far. While the USA was disinterested, China was busy consolidating its regional influence. The country that could have played the part of competing with China, in place of the USA, was Japan. Japan did not exert its presence, and it's diplomacy lacked initiative and creative ideas. However, Prime Minister Hatoyama's 'fraternity' diplomacy may bring another chance for Japan's new diplomatic initiative. In the short term, the competition with the USA and Japan on one side and China on the other side, for having an influence over the regional countries, will be very fierce. If China's 'harmonious world' lasts for the next three years and if Obama's policy initiatives fail to show results, voices calling for new system will rise.

China and Korea have a very close relationship in various areas such as politics, economy, culture and security. Both nations established diplomatic relations in 1992. The status was elevated to 'strategic cooperative partnership', just last year. Both countries are moving towards more mature relations. We must pay attention to at least eight considerations that may influence the future Sino-Korean relationship:-

(i)   Is China's rise today a reality?

(ii)   Will China surpass the USA in the future?

(iii)   What are the contents of Sino-US relations?

(iv)   What kind of power will China be – hegemonic or benign?

(v)   Regional countries' policies towards China.

(vi)   China's position on historical disputes.

(vii)   Will the USA maintain its alliance commitments indefinitely?

(viii) Most importantly, what would be China's role in the process of Korea's reunification i.e. to what extent will China support or oppose reunification?

In the long term, South Korea will take into account all mid to long term factors and its possibilities. Here a favourable posture by the USA and China on the Korean peninsula will become a critical factor for South Korea. However, an important matter for South Korea is not, whether to make a strategic shift but to recongise the changing framework. For the time being Korea's future national strategy will keep the 'alliance' relationship with the USA. At the time when China itself keeps Pyong Yong strategy with the USA, Korea's choosing China would be a risk. It may be unwise to narrow down the range of our own options. However, Korea would like to maintain a strategic cooperative partnership with China and a multilateral security framework. Considering that South Korea's short term China policy has been to elevate the relationship every five years, it is possible that the relationship will again be elevated to a greater status in the year 2013. When a new government comes into office in the year 2013, the two states might consider a comprehensive strategic cooperative partnership. In the next few years, Korea's China policy would not change too much because of reasons such as economic relations and the North Korean nuclear issue. However, ROK-US alliance will be a decisive factor in improving Sino-South Korean relations. This represents a psychological red line.

In order to maximise South Korea's strategic value and to strengthen diplomatic competitive power, South Korea's diplomacy must be extremely flexible. Korea will need to employ multi-dimensional diplomacy. First, since South Korea is an Asian state, it must focus on its relations with other Asian states. Second, Korea must enhance its image as a democratic State by contributing to the international society. Third, it must become a middle power, as a stronghold for North East Asia, with a capacity to influence international consensus. This will reinforce South Korea's strategic value.

Chairman's Remarks

You will note that Professor Hwang has entered the interesting realm of futurology as a prognosis. He has done so in a very scientific manner. Probabilities have been examined and the pronouncements made by him are very sound. We will have to study these very carefully. This is the kind of exercise that all countries in this region need to do. He has also given us a kind of update on China and ROK relations and how it has progressed, and how it is likely to develop.

Session IV : Fourth Paper

Professor Sujit Dutta

My presentation will focus more on politico-strategic issues rather than military issues – hard questions that shape China's rise and its relationship with the rest of Asia. Asia would be the way China sees it. It is essentially seen in terms of its periphery. Defined in terms of neighbourhood, it will cover North-East, East, South-East and Central Asia. That is the kind of milieu in which China's power is rising and that is the kind of milieu on which it will have direct influence as its power grows. There are three or four basic points that shape and reflect the implications of China's rise for Asia.

China's role in the international system has changed dramatically since 1978-79 when the reforms began. As a result of that, the linkages with the West and Japan meant that, a new kind of economic, structural context has come about where China is deeply embedded now in the global supply chains – interdependence has been created. Foreign capital is deeply involved in China and it has now become a central part of the process that runs the world economy in many ways. That is an outcome of the previous 30 years of reform, which China had deliberately chosen. Globalisation has benefitted China and it has deliberately chosen the path of globalisation as part of its reform strategy. It has brought huge gains. GDP, which was about $ 200 billion in 1978-79, has now become $ 2.6 trillion which is about 11 times growth – quite stupendous in terms of purely economic terms. It has added to, from the Chinese perspective, into their overall 'Comprehensive National Power'. China does not see itself as Japan. It sees itself as great power with all kinds of capabilities. Therefore, China's overall strategy is to become a great power and a pre-eminent power in

Asia – a possible peer competitor with the United States. The USA has been a reference point constantly. This has raised dilemmas for them. How much to build? What happens with the nature of American defence expenditure? How much China's defence expenditure should be? These are questions that flow from that kind of goal setting which is to become a peer competitor at some point and to become a greater power. Therefore, the reforms are in a way a strategy to achieve it. Therefore, the globalisation of China, it's entry into different institutions, etc. have their own dynamics. From the Chinese political strategic point of view, they all head towards attaining great power status as early as possible.

No one can deny that China given its size, its civilisational length, its vision of itself, its security context, should become an ultimate power – that is not the question. The question is: *When China tries to become a great power what does it mean to the others who are around it, others who also are either great powers currently or aspire to be one? Principally, four countries are directly affected in this context.* The USA, which is a dominant power and Japan, which is an ally of the USA and a neighbour of China – is directly affected by long years of tussle and tensions. Russia, weakened substantially but nonetheless a power that sees itself as a major Eurasian entity, and finally India. Essentially, the Chinese relationships with these four countries are critically important as it seeks to become a great power. Chinese strategies have to constantly figure out as to how their goal setting affects the national ambitions and goals of these four countries; and the kind of structures and ideologies that others bring to the table. Whether there would be tensions within these goals is something that is critically important. Despite the tensions and historical problems that have existed in many of these relationships, as far as China is concerned, all these powers have helped to make China's rise possible.

China's current reforms and globalisation strategy and growth would not have been possible without the US and Japanese help. That is clear. Americans opened the doors to make possible China's entry into the global system, post-1978-79. The US-China rapprochement was critical to that success and Japan's aid, etc., played a very important role as well. Russians have increasingly helped the Chinese modernisation process, after the Soviet Union collapse. It began during Gorbachev's time itself. India has been a constant supporter of China's entry into the international system – even when our relations were balanced in terms of realist politics. It did not make much sense. But India continued to support China's entry in Security Council, even when the relations were at rock bottom. India accepted Tibet as a part of China when the boundary issue was not settled. Many other examples can be given.

In a situation where these powers are currently engaging China in order to shape the international environment, in which their mutual interests have become integrated and because of globalisation and international cross-border economic linkages, it is very important to maintain stability. China's surge for global power status must keep in mind the interest and the context in which this engagement is taking place. If China continues to surge for equality in terms of military expenditure and other capabilities with the USA it will have a direct implication for the overall stability of this relationship. A comparative defence expenditure kind of viewpoint on missile count and other considerations like dominance of the sea, will have very different implications. It would complicate and make China's overall strategic environment far more difficult. Pursuing this line of thinking will lead to a set of consequences; particularly because, there are significant differences between these four countries – The USA, India, Japan are democracies and in terms of sovereignty – there are problems that exist between India and China, and Japan and China. Because of intended linear projection of power aggrandisement, over time, mutual tensions between these countries have the potential of getting out of hand.

There is a second element to it which is normative in nature, because it follows from ideological and strategic cultures. We all know that there are two strands of traditional Chinese strategic culture – the Confucian and the real politic. It is real politic strategic culture that has dominated Chinese thinking, even though post-Mao years have seen significant modification, in order to make cooperation with the outside world possible. This stand remains, especially within the military and the political establishment; although, there are others within the Chinese establishment, who would like to see increasingly liberalised policies to take place. Nonetheless, the dominant culture appears to be still rooted in realism. In that sense, a competitive 'balance of power' approach, is constantly on the mind of the Chinese. Therefore, 'Comprehensive National Power' and its comparison with the others constantly figure within the strategic community's thinking. There are problems relating to how others perceive the 'peaceful rise' theory or the current theory of 'harmonious world' order. In the context of a normative culture of realism, real politic thinking seems to be on tactical lines rather than strategic long term belief changes. They seem to us to fit into the theory, *'bide your time'*. That is a tactical line rather than a fundamental change in mindset and orientation of ideological position. Ideological change in norms and strategy thinking is essential for establishing a great power and peace over the coming years. There are significant debates taking place within China on this. However, the realist point of view still holds the dominant position.

A third element is China's policy towards its neighbours in Asia. It can be divided into two. One that takes into account, its opposition to the major powers; and the other towards the smaller entities. The smaller entities, which are not in alliance with a major power, have received far more accommodation from the Chinese. Major powers, however, are treated differently and in a far more competitive manner. Given the fact, four important countries have a difficult history with China, means that approaches towards them are to be shaped through a competitive lens. This is visible, for example, in China's approach towards the McMahon Line vis-à-vis Burma and India. Clear discriminatory policy orientations have significantly distorted and created new conditions for difficult relationships.

It should not be said that, changes in relationships have not taken place. We must take note of the positive changes that have taken place in each of these relationships vis-à-vis China. The US-China interaction is recognised as a fundamental relationship of the world. Japan-China relations have turned around – they are now the largest trade partners, and Chinese students are now studying in Japan. India-China relations, ever, since 1988 rapprochement, have flowered despite difficulties. But underlying them are significant tensions. If they are not managed properly, there is a likelihood of a different pathway which could be conflictual in nature, as China's power grows further.

India-China relations are currently based on the 1988 decision to open a new chapter during Rajiv Gandhi's visit to China. One of the elements of that was *'confidence building measures'* i.e. lowering of tensions, peace and tranquility on the border as boundary talks continue to resolve the disputes that exist; and the other *'enhancing stakes in each other's economy'*. Those policies have brought great benefits to the two countries. The essential goal as far as India is concerned, and to a large extent replicated by China, was to maintain long term stability in that relationship. The hope continues to build-up on maintaining a long term India-China stable relationship. Despite that in the last few years, continuously some tensions have emerged. That is mainly because, while this framework has worked well, the elements of dispute resolution, that should have moved along simultaneously, have been stymied. The territorial problems have become even more important, since 1988 when the principles were signed. In 2005 some basic principles were again signed. They were however, not clearly stated. Nonetheless, there were certain benchmarks. One of the principles was, *'keeping the interests of settled populations in mind'* which essentially referred to the Arunachal question. That has now become a flashpoint because the Chinese do not want to have the 'settled population theory' being interpreted in terms of India's sovereignty over Arunachal Pradesh. This has become now a *lietmotif* in Chinese diplomacy.

There is one fundamental problem that the Chinese strategic thinkers and diplomats seem to forget. India's recognition of Tibet as part of China will become null and void if China says Arunachal is Southern Tibet. India cannot wish away its own sovereignty in order to accept Tibet as part of China. So, India's recognition is inbuilt. India's recognition of Tibet, as part of China, can only be meaningful if Arunachal is not considered Southern Tibet. If China continues to mention that Arunachal is Southern Tibet, then the 1954 position goes. The 1954 position in legal terms does not exist. It died in 1962, because that treaty was eight years old. In many ways the Chinese have opened up a Pandora's box by returning to historical questions that were already settled. It has complicated the India-China boundaries settlement further in a manner that the current diplomats and the political class have not realised.

The second element was, meaningful strategic thinking on the Tibetan issue. Both on Taiwan and Tibet, one of the principle of 're-look' is necessary – as far as China is concerned. Because while sovereignty has been accepted by the world, in de facto terms 'Taiwan is independent' and in de facto terms the 'Tibetans are in exile'. Without reaching a deal and an agreement, resolution of the problem is not going to be possible. On the resolution of this hinges great power relationships significantly. In US-China and Japan-China relationships the Taiwan factor is very much central and Tibet question is central to India-China relationship.

'Re-look' on some of these relationships is essential. Political change and ideological make-up regarding old sovereignty stances belonging to pre-colonial and imperial days, cannot be translated into sovereignty control today without accepting the vision, support and will of the people. Therefore, a significant amount of rethink by the strategic community, as far as China's position and the Chinese strategy are concerned is necessary.

Keeping China's relations with Pakistan vis-à-vis India out of the purview of this presentation, it is important to look at: How China wants to shape the strategic environment in South Asia? For example, understanding the consequences of China undermining India's security agreement with Nepal needs a serious study. Without understanding the implications of historical arrangements, there is a likelihood of the relationships getting more complicated.

From here onwards, China has two choices – two pathways. One is to change its notion of becoming a 'great power' through capability building, as well as normative structure build-ups that flow from that kind of old strategic thinking. It needs to carry out a 're-think' on them. If it does not, then there would be one path that would go towards increasing tension and conflictual relations with the other great powers. It may possibly, due to mutual security concerns, lead to a *quasi alliance* between the USA and India – that could be one pathway.

The other pathway would require serious thinking, based on current *interdependencies* that have already been created – in which all the other great powers are willing to cooperate and engage China and move towards it; rather than adopting *unilateral* policy postures for unilateral gains. *Interdependence* would have to be rooted in shared gains, not *unilateral* gains.

Chairman's Remarks

Thank you Professor Dutta for a very lucid and wide ranging presentation. You have attempted to cover the larger picture – a wide sweep that complements the very specific and directed presentations from the other three panelists. The candour with which certain issues have been put on the floor, especially those relating to India-China relations, need attention of all. In an academic discussion, this kind of candour is necessary. These issues are up for 'discussion' and have to be studied through considered research based on a process which would lead to conclusions. That is the conclusion of the presentations by the four panelists. I must compliment

and thank our esteem panellists for the kind of gravity and remarkable way
in which they took on their tasks.

Session IV : Discussion

Issues Raised

In case China implodes, what kind of political system is likely to emerge? What will be the impact of such political changes on China's projected rise in future?

Responses

(a) In China, people are talking about the political direction the country should take, particularly after the collapse of the Soviet Union and Russia giving up on their Communist political ideology. There is a debate on as to what kind of democracy China should follow. They are, however, certain that it would not be western type democracy – like in Hong Kong, Singapore or other parts of the world. They have not yet made up their minds on the choice of alternatives that would suit the Chinese situation. The Chinese common sense is aware that economic growth and political stability would continue to add to their Comprehensive National Power.

(b) The Chinese leadership has been managing the requirement of future reforms very well. They have established a 'successor mechanism' through a coalition among entrepreneurs, politicians and the military, which enjoys popular support. They will not pursue western style political reforms, but are confident of maintaining economic growth and political stability in the near future.

(c) China's peaceful economic and military rise is complementary and would continue to grow to fulfill Chinese aspirations in the 21st Century.

Issues Raised

Are there any changes in the composition of the China Military Commission (CMC) headed by Hu Jintao as the Chairman? Do the high ranking PLA members form a part of the Central Committee also? What role does the PLA play in strategic policy decision making?

Response

In China's political system, it is the Polit Bureau which is at the top and not the CMC. The Standing Committee comprising of nine members is at the top end of the decision making system. In matters related to security the PLA is free to voice their views for consideration by the CMC, but the final decision on all matters is taken by the Standing Committee of the Polit Bureau.

Issue Raised

What will be the role of ethnic minorities in China's pursuit of becoming a great power?

Response

The way China deals with the Uigurs, Tibetans and the Taiwanese is slightly different in each case. Nonetheless, that would be critically important. It would certainly be linked to 'China's rise as a great power', because perception of the world about, whether China would be a responsible power would be determined on the kind of political arrangements it works out with them. In the 21st Century liberal milieu the world needs to know whether the military oriented Communist Party administration would pursue hard line policies or it would choose to have some different kind of identity to conform to current trends on human rights issues.

Issue Raised

How should India interpret the bellicose statements being made by China in recent months? Why is China making such statements against India?

Responses

(a) In the last four years the Arunachal question has come back to the forefront because of the 'ambiguities' that were left in the 2005 Principles. The ambiguities were a result of lack of agreement as consensus could not be achieved. Unlike parts of Aksai Chin, which are not inhabited, Arunachal including Tawang, is a settled area with citizens of India living there. Therefore, the whole situation has to be seen in terms of population and not territory alone. In terms of democratic politics it is 'non-negotiable'. Unlike in the past, an 'imperial' change of territory cannot take place today. The reason this has become such an issue is because the Chinese feel that they are losing their position on their claim on account of democratic politics in Arunachal Pradesh. That is the reason they are stressing their point publicly and in the Asian Development Bank.

(b) With regard to territorial disputes, China accepts some points raised by the Indian side. The problems, however, have arisen because recently Indian side has taken some steps such as the visit of the Prime Minister to Arunachal and allowing the Dalai Lama to visit the area. Since China treats Tibet as a central issue, it is sensitive to any action that undermines Chinese position related to its sovereignty and integrity. Whenever high ranking Chinese officials interact with other countries during their visits, they clearly talk about three No's in Chinese policy :-

(i) No transfer of weapons to Taiwan.

(ii) No meeting with Dalai Lama.

(iii) No supporting of the Xinxiang rebellion forces.

Issue Raised

If three likeminded nations Japan-India-USA (JIUS), arrange to come together to keep out the 'Super Power of 2025' from the arrangements to safeguard trade routes in the Indian Ocean, what would be China's reaction to such an arrangement?

Responses

(a) Under normal circumstances a few countries, even if they are not likeminded, may come together to share the common goal of protecting Sea Lanes of Communication (SLOC) through anti-piracy actions in outer Somalia or Gulf of Aden. China, Japan, Russia, India and South Korea are conducting anti-piracy activities. Such cooperation would come easily for common good. However, it would not be possible to get such cooperation from every country in the region to meet unforeseen emergency situations. That kind of arrangement would work satisfactorily only amongst likeminded countries who share common values and international standards for resolving conflicting interests and issues. In the foreseeable future, there is a possibility of China becoming a likeminded country alongwith Japan and India.

(b) China's naval ships entered the Indian Ocean Region for anti-piracy missions and to counter piracy in maritime area near Somalia. The Chinese realise the urgency and see it as an opportunity to go outside the waters around China. However, they have not figured out their 'two-ocean' strategy as yet. The objective of China's naval activity in this area is very limited. So far, the Chinese decision makers are not sure what to do next. Another issue in this context would be the requirement of financial support for conducting such missions across the Indian Ocean from the Gulf of Aden to Malacca Straits. China has proposed a plan to take care of specific areas but it has not got similar response from other countries as yet.

(c) The idea of dividing zones for controlling piracy is a very recent idea. This is something which is being turned over in the minds of the people. Under the circumstances the best course would be to prepare for the 'worst' but pursue the 'most favourable outcome', and that would take care of everyone's interests and needs.

Issue Raised

China wants its neighbours to keep talking and solve the problems through constant dialogue. However, it is always talking from a position of strength and not equality. For example, take the case with India - despite many meetings, the issues have remained unresolved. In such a situation, how is it possible to continue the dialogue to solve mutual problems?

Response

It is difficult to give a definite answer this question. Diplomatic negotiations are difficult processes in which leverages are brought to bear in order to reach agreements. Therefore, much depends on the kind of leverages India can bring to bear in terms of conditions of gains and losses. At some point of time the solution would happen. However, in between the process, there would be times when crisis can emerge – especially when the territorial and sovereignty issues are involved. The process to agree on certain principles is on in India – the sooner it is in place the better it would be. On China's side there is some rethinking, largely on populated areas. On clearance of this obstacle, India-China territorial question could be settled very soon and very quickly. China's claim on Arunachal will have to be given up as part of an overall settlement on the basis of the position India has taken on Tibet. India has made two fundamental concessions on the table, one, accepting Taiwan as part of a united China and, two, Tibet as part of China. Chinese have not made even a single concession so far.

Issues Raised

To resolve India-China border dispute, both sides should agree in principle to maintain status quo i.e. the *Eastern sector* may continue to be administered by India and the *Western sector* by China leaving aside sovereignty issues. Is it possible to have such arrangements as a basis to start negotiations?

Responses

(a) Starting negotiations, based on this hypothetical proposition would not be correct. The problem with that suggestion is that whereas Aksai Chin in the Western sector has no population, Arunachal Pradesh is a province of India. It is a populated provincial entity with a democratically elected government in full administrative control. The Chinese are objecting unrealistically to the whole democratic process of elected assembly members, Chief Minister and the Prime Minister visiting that area. The administrative situation here is different from Aksai Chin. Therefore, such an anomalous situation as a starting point for the negotiations would not be acceptable.

(b) Prime Minister Nehru made a last desperate attempt to bring peace and goodwill between India and China in 1958. Even our Vice President Hamid Ansari said recently that there is a lot of commonality of interest; there is also a common faith between India and China. Our faith and religion are deep rooted. Study of philology and anthropology also shows similarities in many other things. If political and military leaders on both sides think and ponder over it and talk more of the commonality, then the rest of the world can sleep in peace.

Chairman's Concluding Remarks

The last response from a distinguished member in the audience on India-China relations was 'well said' to wind up the discussions today. The presentations speak for themselves, therefore, it would be superfluous to say anything more. I thank all the panellists for their very thoughtful and stimulating presentations. They have succeeded in generating many issues that would require deep reflection by the distinguished audience to find the right answers. I am aware that perhaps some questions were not answered with the kind of depth and detail they deserved – that is inevitable in all such seminars.

Today, actually the scope of discussion was enlarged beyond the title, 'Building Enduring Power Equations in Asia', and a lot of time was devoted to bilateral India-China relations. That is just as well because this also is part of the larger picture.

I thank you all for your engaged participation and USI for organising this very stimulating and enriching event.

Closing Remarks

Shri Shivshankar Menon, IFS

General PK Singh, Ladies and gentlemen. Thank you for asking me to speak to you and to make some concluding remarks. You have also put me in an awkward position, standing between such fine people and their lunch. I will not even try to summarise what you have done over the last two days, which I think has been very useful. Even to attempt to do so would be a disservice to the speakers and would be impossible given the range of opinions on China that we now display in India, which, I think, is probably more than we ever had before.

I would like to make a few points on what I am taking away from the part of the Seminar that I heard. I don't think we have answered the question in the title of the seminar, namely, whether a rising China is an opportunity or a strategic challenge. To my mind, and from everything I have heard, it is both. It is both an opportunity and a challenge. Over the last day and a half day we have heard much more about the challenges than we did about the opportunities a rising China would create. That is as it should be, given the professions of most of us who are here. I know that every diplomat thinks that he is an armchair general, and every general thinks he knows 'diplomacy' better than the diplomats do. Both of us think that we are 'strategists'. So, this is inevitable – that we will end up stressing the challenges as we did, at the end of this seminar. But for me, it has been a very useful and a very timely exercise because you brought together a range of scholars from around the world of great eminence. The quality of discussion was really quite remarkable.

We seem to be in a China season in New Delhi. This is the fourth high level seminar on China that I have been asked to speak to within less than three weeks time. And, we may be witnessing the emergence of a new national obsession here. For once, and unlike other such phenomena in the past where we have been obsessed with Pakistan, and at certain stages with others, I think that this interest in China is a useful obsession. It is useful and necessary, if it helps to improve our understanding of this phenomenon and our ability to deal with it rationally.

There are also other reasons why I consider it useful, apart from self interest, having tried to study China now for about 40 years. It is useful for Indian scholars to benchmark their work with a comparable society and economy in terms of its size and development imperatives. Undoubtedly, from an Indian point of view, certainly, the rise of China is the most important development in our region and immediate neighbourhood. Since parts of our periphery are also China's periphery, it is inevitable that we will have issues with each other that we have to work our way through quite apart from the bilateral problems which divide us, which were mentioned at various stages, but also larger issues. We will continue to have a relationship between India and China which includes elements of both competition and cooperation. I think that is natural and we might as well accept that rather than getting upset or worried about it.

It would also be a useful obsession if it brought home to us in India our own unique situation and interests, as many of your contributions showed. Sujit Datta of Jamia Milia University was probably the most articulate expression of this. India is both uniquely affected and also uniquely placed to benefit from the rise of China, as many of the points made here showed.

Everybody assumed that we are dealing with a new China; that China's behavior has changed over time. I sometimes wonder whether any power's rise in history has been as carefully studied or foretold as China's. I also hope that the international system is better at understanding and dealing with the rise of China then it has been in previous such cases in history. If we think back over the last five centuries or so the international system has a terrible record of actually dealing with the rise of new powers — whether it was Britain in the 18th Century, the rise of Germany in late 19th or early 20th century, the rise of Japan in 1920's and 30's, and the rise and fall of the Soviet Union. There have also been rises foretold, which have never happened such as Japan in the nineties for instance.

But my own hope, given the quality of discussion here is that this time the international system may have a better chance of understanding and dealing with this particular rise than it did in the past. The reason is simple. It is because the rise of China is unlike any of the other cases I mentioned from the past. Unlike each of those cases, the rise of China is occurring when China is intimately linked to the existing power structure. She is economically bound to the powers that she may replace. Her prosperity, and therefore, regime stability in China itself, seem directly linked through global production chains to the rest of the international system and to other powers. So, China might have developed military capabilities which many of you have to consider professionally through your work. I think the political question must be whether the pattern of China's development and whether events like global economic crisis have de-linked China sufficiently from the rest of the international system and from the West in particular, to open new strategic and political options for her? I am not sure. This is still an open question and I think you heard different answers in the course of the last day and a half from different speakers. (For instance, look at intra-Asian trade where quantity seems to have become quality. Something like 31 per cent of our trade in Asia was intra Asian in 1990, and now we are almost over 50 per cent. The global economic crisis might actually push us over that.)

Secondly, it seems to me that the rise of China is in a sense masking the simultaneous rise of several other powers – South Korea, India, Indonesia to name a few. It is occurring in a very crowded strategic environment, where existing powers like the USA, Japan, Russia regard themselves as Asian powers. We are, therefore, dealing with the rise of Asia but not in the manner in which the West and Europe rose historically. In effect we use the term, the rise of China, as short hand for a much more complex phenomenon which still lacks a name. The fact is that the phenomenon is so much more complex that multiple shifts are occurring at the same time. Theoretically, it should open up opportunities and options for many more powers in the region as the whole system is opening up. There should be more space, theoretically. But that is not what came out of our discussion. This is why I say that we should look more closely at not just the challenges and risks, which we did, but also at the opportunities, at what actually has opened up and what we could be doing together with other powers including China in this emerging situation?

The concentration on challenges rather than opportunities is partly because the rise of China is taking place without any mediatory institutions in place in Asia. Shifts in the balance of power are therefore leading to internal balancing responses – to military build-ups to other things rather than to the cooperative and coordinated kind of actions that you might otherwise expect. Even the external balancing of coalition building that Admiral Kaneda was talking about is not happening.

There is thus, a clear need for some kind of further discussion on the sort of institution building which can provide assurances to all the powers concerned about an increasingly uncertain future. There are two ways of doing so. One is, of course, the Big Bang approach. Prime Minister Rudd gave the clearest expression of that approach by suggesting that we try to set up a pan-Asian institution with a long agenda of all the things we need to do about our cooperative collective security, thus setting up a large regional security architecture. The other way is to begin with practical cooperation; of which anti-piracy operations off the Horn of Africa is a good example, which started practically without any institution in place at all. The institutions developed out of what we were doing. Start small, start with the known, start with the practical, and then build on successful experience. I have suggested elsewhere that one area where a beginning could be made is cooperation in maritime security, from Suez through to the western Pacific. Our own preference has always been for an open security architecture and the sort of multi-polarity that China too advocates in global contexts.

There is space for India and China to grow and manage our relationship successfully, if we both wish it. The question is really that we have a situation where the Asian balance is opening out and we are trying to find a new equilibrium. There are many volunteers for the role of balancer. The US is the first one to put their hand up, but everyone would be happy to be a balancer because everybody else then has to do the hard work. Between India and China, we ourselves have had a bilateral 'modus vivendi' in place since 1988. But like all such 'modus vivendis', it needs to be re-worked periodically, in the light of changes, in India, in China, in the balance around us and in the situation in which we find ourselves.

For us in India, the larger issue is whether India and China can work together to help to manage the complicated regional security environment in Asia. This includes several aspects. One is whether China can deal with partners as equals or whether her hierarchical strategic culture precludes this. Another is whether China and the other rising Asian powers are willing to and capable of providing public goods in terms of security, growth and stability that the continued development of China, India and the region require. China has proved that she can do the economics. Can she also do the politics that come with power? The case in point is whether China can and will help to preserve security in the global commons.

There are many other issues which came up in the course of this discussion. Strategic stability was one which we came close to, but without an answer. But, then like all good seminars, it has left us with more topics for several more seminars and for all of us to meet again.

So, let me congratulate you, General PK Singh and all of you in the

USI, and all the participants who made this a very successful and productive National Security Seminar. I am sure that the seeds you planted here today will bear fruit in the future.

www.ingramcontent.com/pod-product-compliance
Lightning Source LLC
Chambersburg PA
CBHW070810300326
41914CB00078B/1924/J